S0-ABY-827

Spend 90 days on a guided journey through your favorite verses

—ALL TIME—
VERSES
90-DAY SCRIPTURE JOURNEY

A Devotional Edited By

STUDENT MINISTRY SIDEKICK

xulon
PRESS

Copyright © 2013 by Student Ministry Sidekick

ALL TIME VERSES
by Student Ministry Sidekick

Printed in the United States of America

ISBN 9781628715071

All rights reserved solely by the author. The author guarantees all contents are original and do not infringe upon the legal rights of any other person or work. No part of this book may be reproduced in any form without the permission of the author. The views expressed in this book are not necessarily those of the publisher.

Unless otherwise indicated, Bible quotations are taken from the New International Version (NIV). Copyright © 1973, 1978, 1984, 2011 by Biblica, Inc.™. Used by permission. All rights reserved.

www.xulonpress.com

Dedicated to the heroic leaders who shape, guide, and mold a generation of students who will change the world. Thank you for your investment.

• TABLE OF CONTENTS •

• DAY 1 •

Cast all your anxiety on him because he cares for you.
1 Peter 5:7

The epistle of I Peter was written by a man who knew a thing or two about anxiety. If you'll recall, he was the same Peter who, with one step exhibited great faith by walking on water, but with another started sinking because that same faith faltered. Peter understood all too well the deepest, darkest depths of despair and depression when he denied Christ to an enquiring little girl. Peter lived through some dark days, and he knew his readers would need encouragement.

During this time, the church was being persecuted. The Roman Emperor, Nero, set his sights on Christians, wishing to wipe them off the face of the planet. No doubt, many of Peters' readers had lost a loved one to the rampaging Nero. So Peter tells them to cast their cares on Christ.

The word translated for "cast" was used one other place in the New Testament. In Luke 19:35, the Bible describes how the disciples made an improvised saddle for Jesus by casting their outer robes on the back of a donkey. Like the robes, the Holy Spirit is telling us to take all of our cares, anxieties, and worries and give them to Jesus.

Jesus is waiting to take the weight of our worry because He "cares" for us. Our complaints and cares are not grievous to Him. The God of the impossible is waiting to be invited into our impossible situations.

The word for "cares" conjures up the idea of an investor. Meaning, like a financial investor watching the stock market, God is intently focused on His investment: us.

TODAY'S CHALLENGE
- Are you concerned about finances? Then go to the One who owns "the cattle on a thousand hills." (Ps 50:10)
- Are you worried about what tomorrow may bring? Then trust in the God Who's already there. (Matt. 6:25).
- Have you lost your faith? Then ask Jesus to help you find it again. (Mark 9:24)
- Do you feel burdened with an impossible weight? Then "Cast all your anxiety on Him because He cares for you."

Ben Hyrne • Student Pastor • Calvary Baptist Church, GA

• DAY 2 •

Therefore, "Come out from them and be separate," says the Lord.
"Touch no unclean thing, and I will receive you."
2 Corinthians 6:17

The word "separation" is often made synonymous with "isolation," and understandably so. For instance, a metallurgist makes his living on isolating and extracting compounds to purify metals such as gold and silver. If you were to look on the inside of a wedding band, you would see a mark indicating the degree of purity. It might say "14K," or it might even say "24K," the purest state of gold we're able to manufacture. The more "isolated" the gold, the more valuable it is.

Like gold, too many Christians believe they will be more valuable to God if they were to isolate themselves from the world. They feel that every acquaintance they purposefully drive away purifies their walk with God. The sad thing is, not only have they forgotten the price God has already paid for them, but they've also equated moral separation with social isolation. Meaning, they think, "The more isolated I am the more righteously pure I am." This should not be.

We are called to be morally separated, but socially integrated. Jesus said in Matthew 5:13, "You are the salt of the earth." Much like gold, salt is extracted and purified. But unlike gold, salt is not meant to be adored for its purity and isolated for fear of tarnishing. Instead, it is meant to be integrated in foods and consumed. Salt is used to bring flavor to an otherwise flavorless meal.

We are salt. We are the ingredient that brings life to an otherwise decaying world. To isolate ourselves would mean leaving a decaying world to rot.

Paul was not proposing we isolate ourselves from the world. He was gauging his readers' saltiness. He was challenging them to look into their own lives and ask, "How salty am I? Have I lost my distinctiveness? Have I become ineffective in my desire to be socially isolated; or, am I engaging the lost? Does the world even notice the difference between me and them?"

TODAY'S CHALLENGE
The world needs to see the Word of God fleshed out in the people of God for the purpose of God.

- What have you allowed in your life that has made you lose your Christian distinctiveness?
- What can you do to promote a Christ-centered life instead of Self-centered life?

Ben Hyrne • Student Pastor • Calvary Baptist Church, GA

• DAY 3 •

"Come, follow me," Jesus said, "and I will send you out to fish for people".
Matthew 4:19

"Fishing is boring, unless you catch an actual fish, and then it is disgusting." – Dave Barry

Have you ever been fishing? If so, maybe you feel like Mr. Barry. Fishing is a waste of time to you, unless you actually catch something. At least if you catch a fish there is some excitement, but even then it can get messy. Fish can be slimy, squirmy and smelly. You may get wet, and you may be using live bait like minnows, crickets or worms. If you keep the fish for food later, then you have to clean the scales and cook it.

Many Christians feel the same about telling others about Jesus. They think it's boring and a waste of time because no one is actually going to believe what they are saying. If someone does seem interested in knowing more about Jesus, it can get kind of messy with questions they may ask and answers you may not have at that moment. It would be easier and a lot less sticky to attend church and do the occasional quiet time than to fully trust Christ and the mission He has for all believers in sharing the Gospel.

Just like He did with the disciples in Matthew, Jesus calls us to follow Him. He calls Christ followers to move past their ordinary life and to embrace a life spent drawing closer to God and His promises. He also calls us to share Jesus with others by how we act and what we say. He instructs a believer to go fishing. Unlike actual fishing, Christians are not using bait to trick non-believers into false hope or promises, but we are simply sharing with non-believers the same love and grace that radically changed our life.

- Where are some places you can go "fishing?"
- What are some ways you can prepare to go "fishing?"
- Who is someone you know needs to know more about Jesus?

TODAY'S CHALLENGE
Father, give me courage today to go "fishing." Help me to fully trust Your promises and obey Your commands. Let my actions and words draw people to You today.

Chris Rainey • Associate and Student Pastor • Liberty Baptist Church, GA

• DAY 4 •

Do not be anxious about anything, but in every situation, by prayer and petition, with thanksgiving, present your requests to God. And the peace of God, which transcends all understanding, will guard your hearts and your minds in Christ Jesus.
Philippians 4:6-7

"Why hasn't he texted me back yet? It's been like 2 minutes already, and he liked one of Ashley's Instagram pictures since my text!"

"My parents are fighting, and I heard them talking about divorce. What's going to happen to my family?"

"There is so much to do with school, homework, sports, work and time with friends and family. I can't handle how busy I am right now!"

Worry has a way of taking over a life. Whether it is in relationships at school, or at home, worry always seems to be there ready to flood your life. It's hard not to worry when life is spinning out of control. Friendships are breaking down; you are fighting with your parents; or you are simply too busy to handle every single thing at the moment. It is a hopeless feeling. How can we overcome worry?

We give it to God.

It sounds so easy, but it can be so hard to do. We go to God so often as a last resort when it should be the first thing we do. When worry begins to creep in, stop what you are doing and pray. Instead of allowing doubts to race in your mind, take time to tell God what is worrying you and ask for His help. Thank God that He is listening and that He is going to take care of you through this tough situation.

When we trust God with the issues we are dealing with, His peace guards us. No longer is worry flooding our life, but God's peace becomes our shield and protection from the rising waters. It's not that God takes us out of those situations, but that He gives everything we need to endure those hard times. When we pray we are trusting that God is in control, and He will take care of us. When we trust, we find peace, even in the fiercest storms.

TODAY'S CHALLENGE
Today, when you start to stress about something, pray this: "Father, I trust you with (the issue). Do what you think is best. Thank you for hearing my prayers and for caring for me. Amen."

Chris Rainey • Associate and Student Pastor • Liberty Baptist Church, GA

• DAY 5 •

But in your hearts revere Christ as Lord. Always be prepared to give
an answer to everyone who asks you to give the reason for the hope that you have.
But do this with gentleness and respect
1 Peter 3:15

Hope. It's a word that would have resonated deeply with the recipients of Peter's letter. Nero was currently reigning in Rome and his persecution of Christians had probably rippled to Northern Asia Minor where the recipients of this letter resided. Confused and discouraged by this hostile environment, hope was scarce and desperately needed.

When addressing the believers, Peter does not appeal to a hope that stems from improvement in circumstances. Instead, he calls the believers to a response in the midst of their circumstances. He calls them to revere or set apart Christ as Lord. He calls them (and us!) to remember that our Lord is in control. Even in suffering, our Lord is sitting on the throne and our hope is unchanging.

Like the church in Northern Asia Minor, however, the reason for our hope cannot be in our circumstances. The recipients of Peter's letter would have known and felt this deeply in the midst of their trying circumstances. Even today we are repeatedly reminded of this truth. Whether it's a shattered dream, broken marriage or job layoff – over and over we find circumstances an unreliable foundation for our hope.

Our hope, therefore, is in the life, death and resurrection of Jesus Christ. This hope is unfailing for God has provided a guaranteed way for us to have a relationship with Him and He has proven to us that He has the power to conquer death. Though circumstances in life may look despairing, we can cling to God's promise that He will return and will make all things right.

As much as we continue to need this hope, those who surround us also desperately need it. Be a voice of hope in a world that is searching for a place of refuge. And speak with gentleness and respect so that those who hear you may be drawn to listen!

TODAY'S CHALLENGE
God, help me remember that my hope is founded on Christ, not in my circumstances. Prompt me to share this hope with everyone that I encounter.

Katie Jones • Minister in Residence • First Baptist Woodstock, GA

• DAY 6 •

*If we confess our sins, he is faithful and just and will forgive us our sins
and purify us from all unrighteousness.*
1 John 1:9

Sin. It's an uncomfortable subject. In church, we all nod our heads and agree. Sin is wrong and yet it is everywhere we look. Often, though, we are so busy pointing out the sins of others that we flippantly brush ours aside. We rationalize our sin and go through the motions with the reasoning that "no one is perfect." We dismiss our harshly spoken words and our insistence on our own way as no big deal.

The truth is, however, that while we are quick to point out the sin in our culture, we live in denial of our own. 1 John 1:9, however, is primarily addressing not the world – but us. We may choose to live in denial of our sin, but God does not. He has called us out of denial. He has called us to confession.

The self-examination preceding confession can be discouraging. It shatters the façade of the perfection we long for and confronts us with our brokenness. It reminds us of who we want to be, but are not. Yet ironically when we refuse to confess, we lose. We miss out on the invitation to know the depth of our need for Jesus, the invitation to love Him more.

Our Savior is faithful and just. Though our self-examination may cause us to cringe, He does not shy away. As believers, we can come before Him with confidence. This confidence does not stem from the idea that our pride, selfishness or unthankfulness is "not all that bad" but a confidence based on Christ's sacrifice. We are assured forgiveness not because of who we are, but because of who He is.

Confession is not punishment. God does not benefit in any way when we admit our wrong. Confession is for our good. It refines us as it reminds us who God is and of our need for a Savior. It reminds us of our hope in the One who works righteousness in us – a work He has promised to finish (Phil. 1:6).

TODAY'S CHALLENGE
God, I admit I often live in denial of my sin. Help me to be quick to confess it, knowing I am forgiven because of who You are.

Katie Jones • Minister in Residence • First Baptist Woodstock, GA

• DAY 7 •

Therefore, my dear brothers and sisters, stand firm. Let nothing move you.
Always give yourselves fully to the work of the Lord, because you know that
your labor in the Lord is not in vain.
1 Corinthians 15:58

"Work hard!" We have all heard a parent, teacher, or coach tell us this. They are telling us to keep trying and to give our best effort to an assignment, a chore, or a sport. Sometimes they are telling us this because we will be in trouble if we do not complete the task and sometimes they are telling us to give our best effort because of the reward that we will receive at the end of the class or end of the season.

Paul was telling the Christians at Corinth to keep working hard and to keep living for God. He encouraged them to do so as a result of their faith in God. He told them to not quit because God was going to reward them for their diligent labor. This verse comes at the end of a great chapter about the certainty of eternal life because of Christ's resurrection. They should work hard and live for God even when it was difficult because Christ has risen and heaven is real.

Today, we need to hear the same message. Don't give up. Don't quit. Resist temptation. Shine as a light and share the gospel. It is worth it! Give your all for God because God rewards those that live for him. No matter what you face today, you can know that living for God is worth what it will cost you. Living for God will often cost you more than you think, but it will reward you more than you can ever imagine.

TODAY'S CHALLENGE
God, when I am tempted to quit, help me to remember that Christ has risen and that a life lived for you is worth whatever it may cost.

Jason Mitchell • Pastor of Outreach and New Initiatives • First Baptist Springfield, VA

• DAY 8 •

The Lord is my light and my salvation—whom shall I fear? The Lord is the
stronghold of my life—of whom shall I be afraid?
Psalm 27:1

Fear. We all have it. Maybe you are scared of spiders, high places, or close spaces. Fear is real and it is personal. Others may not understand what you fear and may even mock you for your fears, but fear does not have to be ignored and it does not have to cripple your walk with God and life for Him in the world.

In this verse, David writes and compares the fears he has to the faithfulness that God has shown him. While you may not fear armies surrounding you (like he does in the next two verses), when you stare at your own situation, your fear may seem inescapable and unconquerable. Instead of staring at your situation, you need to stare at the faithfulness of the God who brings light, deliverance, and salvation. David knows that God brings salvation and he is resting in God's faithfulness despite all of the turmoil that surrounds him.

God does not always rescue us from troubling situations, but He will always be with us in them. The next time you begin to fear, remember that God has given you the most important thing you ever need: salvation through Jesus Christ. Additionally, remember that you are not alone in the situation and that God wants to be your stronghold or place of shelter in your times of trouble. When fear strikes, do not stare at the situation; praise the God of your salvation and remember how He has worked so faithfully in your life in the past. There is no opponent or situation that compares to the greatness of our God!

TODAY'S CHALLENGE
Lord, when I am tempted to fear, help me to look at you, the great God of my salvation instead of the troubles of my situation.

Jason Mitchell • Pastor of Outreach and New Initiatives • First Baptist Springfield, VA

• DAY 9 •

For God did not give us a spirit of timidity, but a spirit of power,
of love, and of self-discipline.
2 Timothy 1:7

Timidity is a synonym for fear, which is something that each and every person experiences in his or her life. Some people are even fear enthusiasts and seek out various opportunities to face their fears. For example, you can watch horror movies, enter "haunted" houses, and even get into a shark cage and face a great white shark toe to toe – or teeth to teeth. People willingly choose to face their fears to overcome and move beyond them, but fear is not something that God gives you.

- What fears have you allowed into your life?
- How do you allow these fears to impact your daily life as a Christ follower?

God has not given us a spirit of timidity, but He has given us character qualities that will strengthen our faith. God gives us a spirit of power, which makes us stronger than we think we are. It means that we are powerful when we are on the shoulders of God. We have His mighty power working in our lives so that we can overcome anything we encounter. God has given us a spirit of love too. He has given us compassion and affection for others, which He demonstrates through Jesus' death on the cross. God forgives our sins because He loves us and we should forgive others because we love God and care for those whom He loves.

God also gives us a spirit of self-discipline, which extends from the power and love He has given us. Our self-discipline is only as strong as our love for God and desire to see His power work in our lives. We must discipline ourselves to glorify God in our actions, speech, and thoughts because we love Him.

- How has God shown His power to you during your times of trouble?
- Do you love others the way God loves you? How do you show this love?
- How do you demonstrate your self-discipline on a daily basis?

TODAY'S CHALLENGE
Lord, give me the power to overcome the fears I have let impact my life. Lead me to love others like you love me and to be disciplined in how I act, speak, and think.

Scott Huff • Student Pastor • Coastal Community, SC

• DAY 10 •

I have fought the good fight, I have finished the race, I have kept the faith.
2 Timothy 4:7

In today's culture, it seems that everything is a competition, including school, careers, social standing, and even spiritual maturity. We are constantly comparing ourselves to others to see where we stand. When we are losing out to someone else we begin to seek out ways to catch up and win, sometimes no matter what the cost may be. We see this play out today in politics, sports, and business transactions where people do not fight the "good" fight but fight immorally and unethically.

1. How have you seen people competing with immoral and unethical methods?
2. What motivates you to fight the "good" fight?

As a follower of Jesus, you are fighting the battles of life, in which God asks you to fight daily with pure methods. The world tells you to do whatever it takes to win because it's all about you and your status. Paul says in this verse to "keep the faith", meaning to remain faithful to the teachings of Jesus, who teaches us to glorify God with our lives. If we are succeeding in life because we lie, cheat, and steal, then we are not glorifying God with our lives, because these things go directly against His Word.

There comes a point in your life when you have to decide how you want to live your life. You will have to choose between keeping the faith and abandoning it for worldly reasons. Remaining faithful is about perseverance and holding on to God's words. It means that you continually choose to rely on and obey God because He is your ultimate prize and the finish line is at His feet. Commit to running the race set before you in a way that shows your commitment to the teachings of Jesus.

Will you leave your faith behind you because you think success cannot be achieved with it? How will you choose to run your race of life?

What guidelines do you need to set up for yourself so that you will run with your faith?

TODAYS CHALLENGE
Lord, fill my heart with a desire to glorify you alone. I want to live a life of obedience to your Word that reflects my commitment to faith in you.

Scott Huff • Student Pastor • Coastal Community, SC

• DAY 11 •

I praise you because I am fearfully and wonderfully made; your works are wonderful, I know that full well. My frame was not hidden from you when I was made in the secret place, when I was woven together in the depths of the earth.
Psalm 139:14-15

Praise. When we talk to God, this would be the opposite of what we too often do. Complain. What a bold move to call a lot of people out on that. I do this way too often, offering complaints about all the injustice in my life more often than praises. If we look at the Scripture above, we see two main reasons why our proper response each day should be praise. First of all, God made us with great care and purpose. The psalmist says, "fearfully and wonderfully made." The God of the universe made us with great care, but not only that, He remained fearful while creating us. This means that He was very meticulous in his craftsmanship.

Think about it. The God who spoke the world into motion also took careful time to knit us together. Second of all, God's great love warrants praise. Our frame was not hidden from him, according to the psalmist. This proves that God did not turn a blind eye and just let nature take its course, so to speak. Instead, he loved us so much wove each one of us together. Too often do we complain to our Creator rather than praise Him. Let this be a charge to see just how much God cares for us. Everything we do is a response to the Lord.

The question is, will we respond with praise as we realize all that God has done for us even before we were born? We know what the right action is, and hopefully these few words will show how much of an honor it is to praise our true Father.

TODAY'S CHALLENGE
We respond to our Creator daily in one of two ways: praise or complaint. God loves us. Respond with praise.

Josh Reid • Student Pastor • First Baptist Cary, NC

• DAY 12 •

If anyone forces you to go one mile, go with them two miles.
Matthew 5:41

Think about what you need to do today. You might need to go to work, or you might be home putting off that lawn mowing you know is calling your name. We have several things to do in life and a short while to do them. This particular verse touches on the attitude while doing the task rather than the task at hand.

If someone asks you to do something, as a believer, you have an opportunity not to just simply complete the task, albeit that remains the correct thing to do, but to do that task with great excellence. If a coach of a football team were to ask a player to continue lifting weights in the gym and that player merely lifted for an hour a day then yes, he did the job accordingly. However, the superstar player does not only work out, but he also does position-specific drills that will increase his affinity for something he has done his whole life. You see, there is a major difference between good and great. When someone asks you to do something, do it to the best of your ability, as well as you can, with the best attitude possible. Within Scripture, we see numerous examples of those who did what they were called to do even to extreme points. Paul was thrown into prison for preaching the Gospel, but not only that, he willed to die for his faith.

Whether mowing the grass, conversing with a client, or whatever else you must do, do so with great excellence and willingness to do more than originally asked. Ask yourself these questions today. Am I doing what I am supposed to do with the correct attitude in mind? Am I glorifying God with my attitude surrounding the task at hand, willing to go the extra mile?

TODAY'S CHALLENGE
We have an opportunity to display Christ with excellence. Go the extra mile to be sure that happens today.

Josh Reid • Student Pastor • First Baptist Cary, NC

• DAY 13 •

But I tell you: Love your enemies and pray for those who persecute you.
Matthew 5:44

One of the toughest lessons I had to learn, as a teenager growing up, was that God loves everyone equally. I knew John 3:16 said, "God so loved the world", but I wasn't sure His love included the people in my life who were mean, nasty, spiteful and hurtful.

- Have you ever felt this way?

I can remember growing up hearing my pastor say, "As Christians, we don't have the privilege of being mean or getting even." WHAT!? All I wanted to do was lash out at my enemy when they said hurtful things. I would get so frustrated thinking, "Why must I be the loving one? Can't my fist be love and we'll call it 'hard love'?" I couldn't, however, deny what God's Word said. I remember one day reading Mark 8:34, "Whoever wants to be my disciple must deny themselves and take up their cross and follow me." I made a decision that day; if God was willing to die for me, then I can deny my desire to fight back. I decided I would obey His Word, even if that meant loving my enemies.

- So how do I love my enemies?

"If your enemy is hungry, feed him; if he is thirsty, give him something to drink. In doing this, you will heap burning coals on his head. Do not be overcome by evil, but overcome evil with good."(Romans 12:20-21) I soon began to apply this passage and it worked! Instead of returning fire with fire, I would let the hurtful remark go. My enemy would soon see that my interest was no longer 'blow for blow,' but rather how I could love or serve them in spite of their meanness.

God's Word says in Matthew 5:5 "Blessed are the meek, for they will inherit the earth." Meekness means: power under control. Learning what to say and how to act can be a powerful thing. If you can learn to control both, that is true power!

TODAY'S CHALLENGE
Lord, may I honor you today by the words I say and the things I do. Let Psalm 37:11 ring in my heart, "the meek will inherit the land and enjoy peace and prosperity." Help me to love my enemies, the way you do.

Robby Lewis • Student Pastor • The Journey Church, FL

• DAY 14 •

When the woman saw that the fruit of the tree was good for food and pleasing to the eye, and also desirable for gaining wisdom, she took some and ate it. She also gave some to her husband, who was with her, and he ate it.
Genesis 3:6

Have you ever been traveling on your 'normal route' to school...work...home...and saw something you'd never seen before? You said to yourself, "Has that always been there? I can't believe I've never seen that." You begin to point 'it' out to others; you might even begin to focus and be very meticulous about whatever that 'thing' is. Soon you find yourself looking more at that 'thing' than you do the road ahead.

- Has this ever happened to you?
- What's drawing your focus today?

As we look back at the story of Adam and Eve, we can see that they knew of the "tree of knowledge of good and evil," but in verse 6 we learn that knowledge became infatuation because of deception. "The woman saw that the fruit of the tree was good for food and pleasing to the eye..." This was not the first time they would've seen this tree, but now their glance became a stare. They were deceived with thoughts of "wisdom" and power. Their focus shifted from the blessings of Eden and all that God had provided for them, to a desire for something more.

Sin is so often like this. It begins with a glance, and then turns into a gaze, then a stare and before we know it we're consumed by that thought. Can you imagine how different things would've been if Adam and Eve would've talked to God about this tree? God's Word says, "You covet but you cannot get what you want, so you quarrel and fight. You do not have because you do not ask God" (James 4:2).

- How often do the things of this world distract you?
- Are you losing focus of God's provision and plan for your life?
- When is the last time you asked God for wisdom? Clarity? Direction?

TODAY'S CHALLENGE
Lord, lead me today and let me follow You. Help me to focus on the road ahead. Empower me to look beyond any distractions in my life that would take my focus away from You.

Robby Lewis • Student Pastor • The Journey Church, FL

• DAY 15 •

Give thanks in all circumstances; for this is God's will for you in Christ Jesus.
1 Thessalonians 5:18

We all experience highs and lows; there is no way around it. As followers of Christ, we are called to "give thanks in all circumstances." We live in a society that teaches individuals to lean on one another in times of need, times of stress, and times of fear. There is nothing wrong with leaning on individuals to help build and lift you up. However, the problem is that society teaches people to lean on others first rather than God.

In my own life, there have been times that I have felt alone, afraid, and unsure of what lies ahead. But in those times, I stop and converse with the Lord t0 seek His will for me. God ultimately has a plan and purpose for everything. Regardless of the personal effects of the outcome, God can use it for good in some way.

We live in an unsure age in regards to politics, the economy, the job sector and security, but there is always one place you can seek assurance; God! Do not fear and do not be anxious for God will surely strengthen you and uphold you because He is a righteous, loving, and compassionate Father.

No matter what is going on in your life and regardless of the level of stress that you may be feeling or the anxiousness and fear that is present, drop to your knees and converse with God. Begin with prayer. Give thanks for what you have rather than letting the situation consume you. If you are stressed at school, be thankful God has provided you with the ability and opportunity to be educated. If you are having medical issues, be thankful that God is an all-powerful God who can heal all things. There is nothing too great that He cannot handle!

TODAY'S CHALLENGE
Take a minute and sneak off to the restroom, take a drive, or do whatever you have to do to get away. Then consider all the things that you are truly grateful for. It will be impossible not to sense a change of attitude as you put your problems in perspective with a different lens on!

Chris Fedorcek • Young Adults Pastor • Sanctuary of Ocala, FL

• DAY 16 •

For we live by faith, not by sight.
2 Corinthians 5:7

To tell you the grass is green and the sky is blue is not something you will debate and lose sleep over because you see it, and it's right in front of you. You believe it and accept it based on the evidence you can see. This is the struggle for many in today's society in regards to truly living out one's faith. Our society tends to find it a necessity to see before we believe. The problem with this notion is that it's not biblical.

Hebrews 11:1 gives a clear biblical definition of faith; "Now faith is confidence in what we hope for and assurance about what we do not see." Some translations use the word "conviction," which is simply a "fixed or firm belief," instead of "assurance." It is something that cannot be tainted regardless of the argument put forth against it.

It is by faith that we experience true freedom and relationship with Christ. In John 20:29 Christ says, "Because you have seen me, you have believed; blessed are those who have not seen and yet believe." It is "through faith" in Christ and Christ alone that we are saved, not by our own doing and surely not by placing our faith in the things or people of this world.

Are you putting your faith in things or people that continually fail you and fail to provide any feeling of completeness? The answer to this question will reveal a lot about where your heart is and make clear where your faith truly lies.

It is my prayer that you open your heart to the Lord and place your faith in Him and Him alone for He will never forsake you nor lead you towards a path of destruction. True faith will free you to experience a life with Christ to its fullest!

TODAY'S CHALLENGE
Father, grant me clarity and strength to break away from the things of this world in which I put my faith. Open my eyes and my heart to the truth that only through you can I experience a complete and joyous life!

Chris Fedorcek • Young Adults Pastor • Sanctuary of Ocala, FL

• DAY 17 •

Religion that God our Father accepts as pure and faultless is this: to look after orphans and widows in their distress and to keep oneself from being polluted by the world.
James 1:27

"I'm sorry, Mr. Clamp. Your son, Grayson, is totally deaf." Len and his wife, Nicole, sat speechless as they heard the results of the unsuccessful cochlear implant. In Grayson's first three years of life he had already faced open heart surgery, blindness in one eye, total deafness, and abandonment.

Len and Nicole took James 1:27 seriously, obeyed Jesus, and became foster parents. Grayson was their fifth child they fostered, and he came to them directly from the hospital after undergoing heart surgery. His biological mother gave up parental rights shortly after, and Len and Nicole were faced with a decision to adopt. They never planned to adopt, but God has a way of changing plans.

A few months after they received the discouraging news about his hearing, they received an unexpected call from Grayson's audiologist. He had chosen Grayson to be the first child in the US for an experimental surgery to implant a device directly on the brain that by-passed the ear. It would involve risky brain surgery, but could potentially restore Grayson's hearing and give him the ability to communicate with the world.

A month after the brain surgery, Len sat in a small sound booth behind Grayson as he played with a toy. The audiologist nodded to indicate that he had turned on the device. Len said, "Grayson, it's your Daddy." Grayson's eyes widened, and he froze. He slowly lifted his head and then a big smile came on his face as turned to look into the face of his father. His father's voice would be the first words he ever heard.

Is your heavenly Father speaking to you? What does he want you to do? His commands are not burdensome, but a privilege to partner with God as He restores and redeems a broken world. What part will you play in finding a home for every foster child or orphan in your community? Maybe He wants to use you to bring someone into God's family. Don't be hesitant to obey. Who knows? You may find yourself in the middle of a miracle.

TODAY'S CHALLENGE
Spend ten minutes in quiet solitude before God. Ask Him to speak to you today about whatever is on your heart.

Lee Clamp • Director of Evangelism • South Carolina Baptist Convention

• DAY 18 •

If anyone, then, knows the good they ought to do and doesn't do it, it is sin for them.
James 4:17

You know you are from the south when you turn eight years old and your grandfather gives you a shotgun. My son, Caden, could hardly contain himself when he received his first shotgun, and after much practice and instruction, we went on a deer hunt. It will be a day we will never forget.

We stood on the edge of the woods, and I whispered to Caden, "The deer will come right out in front of us if the dogs jump one. Aim for the shoulder and pull the trigger. I promise that I will give you the first shot." If I had known what was about to come out of the woods, I would not have made that promise.

We heard the dogs barking and then the biggest buck I have ever seen bounded out of the pines. My mouth dropped and we quickly put the guns up to our shoulders. This was no time to teach Caden the importance of keeping your word, but I decided to keep my promise.

As the buck ran just 40 yards in front of us, all I could think was, "Pull the trigger, Caden, and then I am going to unload on this beast!" Caden waited...and waited...and waited. In my head I'm screaming, "Pull the TRIGGER!!" As the deer turned to run away from us, Caden finally shot. Then, I shot 5 times, but it was too late.

God is not impressed that you know what you are supposed to do. He wants you to pull the trigger and DO what you are supposed to do. Which is worse, to be a raging alcoholic or to know the cure for alcoholism and keep silent? To be filled with lust or to know the source of true love and not share it? To be a liar or to know the truth and not tell it? Don't waste any more opportunities. Pull the trigger!

Ten minutes later, three deer ran toward us. Caden pulled the trigger, and with 1 shot, he killed his first deer. I yelled out, "You got one!" He looked up at me and said, "Get the rest of them!" It took me 5 shots, but we took two deer home that day. Pull the Trigger!

TODAY'S CHALLENGE
Take a few minutes and confess to God an area of your life that you know is sin and have chosen to dishonor God. Then ask God to give you a chance today to honor Him by doing the right thing.

Lee Clamp • Director of Evangelism • South Carolina Baptist Convention

• DAY 19 •

He made Him who knew no sin to be sin on our behalf, so that we might
become the righteousness of God in Him.
2 Corinthians 5:21

Have you ever had anyone "take the fall" for you? Many in our culture take a lot of pride in not being a "snitch," or in kindergarten terms, a "tattletale," even if it means facing consequences that our friends deserve. The ability to take the fall for someone shows that we possess toughness as well as a great love or respect for that person. But, there is something about every human that will allow us to only fall so far before we point to the guilty party.

- Have you ever taken on someone else's guilt, even in the most minor circumstance?
- Is it hard to take on someone else's guilt when you know you're innocent?

Jesus did more than just take on our guilt. Paul says in 2 Corinthians that Jesus become something that he hated so that we could become something that we could never be on our own. It's amazing to think about Jesus becoming our sin. He didn't just take the punishment of our sin. He took on full ownership of our sin. In that moment while Jesus was hanging on a cross, He became the focal point of every ounce of God's wrath. Why?

Jesus became our sin so that we could become the righteousness of God! He became our worst so that we could become His best! Jesus didn't just die so that we could escape Hell. Jesus died so that we could live out His righteousness….His goodness, His love, His humility, His reflection.

Can you honestly say that your life reflects Jesus righteousness? How are you being like Christ in your love for people, your choices, your relationship with your parents, etc.?

Are there areas in your life in which you are not living out God's righteousness? Identify the choices and sin in your life that Christ chose to become so that you could be forgiven and ask Him to forgive you and help you turn from those today

---

TODAY'S CHALLENGE
Lord, Help me to not cheapen your sacrifice by living a life doesn't reflect who you are. Help me to always remember the price you paid…not just so I can get to heaven, but so that I can live for you NOW.

Stephen Fountain • Student Pastor • First Baptist Buford, GA

• DAY 20 •

By this all men will know that you are my disciples, if you have love for one another.
John 13:35

I love watching people enter a space full of other people. Whether it is a stadium, a gym, a classroom, a park, or a church, the number one goal is always to identify with a certain group. It may mean wearing neon to fit in with the student section at a football game or wearing a flat-billed hat to let everyone know you are a baseball player. You want people to know you are something...whatever you may be. But how often do we think, "How do people know that I'm a follower of Jesus?"

- How often do you think about how you love others, especially other Jesus followers?
- Do people recognize that you are a follower of Jesus because of the way you treat other people?

Jesus presented His disciples with an extremely simple, but unnatural statement. He says that people will know they are His followers not by the clothes they wear, the church they go to, or the words they say, but they will know by their LOVE. Love, selfless desire for God's best for those around us, is the opposite of how we are wired. Jesus says that our Love is what sets us apart from the rest of the world. Love is how we are identified as Christ followers.

We are able to love because Jesus loves us. He loves us so much that He gave His life for us, and He expects us to do the same for others. We are his reflection in the world, and He is love. Like a child inherits blue eyes from his blue-eyed dad, we inherit love for one another from a loving God.

Are there people in your family, on your team, at your school, or at your church that are hard to love? If so, will actively loving them allow you to identify even more with Jesus than loving those who are easy to love?

Do people know you are a follower of Jesus by the way you treat others?

TODAY'S CHALLENGE
Lord, help me to love others, especially my brothers and sisters in Christ, selflessly and unconditionally so that it is clearly evident that I am a follower and reflection of Jesus. Let my love for people point others to You!

Stephen Fountain • Student Pastor • First Baptist Buford, GA

• DAY 21 •

But you are a chosen people, a royal priesthood, a holy nation, God's special possession, that you may declare the praises of him who called you out of darkness into his wonderful light.
1 Peter 2:9

Who are you? Unfortunately, often times, our answer to that question is directly tied to what we do. We allow what we do to determine who we are. We answer that question, "I'm a teacher, I'm a student, I'm a banker, I'm a pastor..." and in that mentality, we allow that profession to define who we are. In reality, who we are, our identity, ought to lead us to do what we do.

- How would you answer the question, "who are you"?
- In what ways do you allow your profession to define you?

In this verse, we are given a clear identity of who we are followed by a clear call of what we are to do. Who we are determines what we do not the other way around! Who are you? As a follower of Jesus, you are a chosen people. You are apart of a people that is much greater than just you! This is bigger than the individual! You are a royal priesthood! You are ROYALTY! You are apart of the priesthood of believers- again bigger than just you! You are a Holy Nation! God demands you to live holy lives, to pursue and seek to be holy. Your life must look different than those who do not profess Jesus! You're HOLY! The last one is my favorite. You're God's special possession. You're HIS! You are God's possession. What could ever happen to you that God hasn't already worked out in the end? Despite what you've done, and where you've been, He looks at you, and says "You're MINE." You're Gods possession---that is who you are.

As a chosen people, royal priesthood, holy nation, and as God's possession you are called to declare His praises, specifically that He has called you out of the darkness and into the light. Has God called you out of the darkness and into the light? If so, then you are His possession and your job is to declare His praises. You are to tell people what God has done in your heart, and in your life. Who you are always leads into what you do, and as God's chosen possession, we are to declare His praises. Go and tell someone about the greatness of our God.

TODAY'S CHALLENGE
Lord, help me to see that I am your possession and nothing can ever change that. I am who you say I am, and as a result of that I will declare your praises of how you have called me out of the dark and into the light!

Mike D'Attoma • Student Pastor • First Baptist Barnwell, SC

• DAY 22 •

For we are God's handiwork, created in Christ Jesus to do good works,
which God prepared in advance for us to do.
Ephesians 2:10

In our image-saturated culture, the way someone looks leads people to believe certain things about them. We are a culture that is influenced highly by what we see on television and in the movies. Our culture is saturated with "you must to do this to be popular, or look like this, or dress like this..." and the unfortunate reality is that often times this mentality carries over into the church. Often times, we look into the mirror and we see nothing of value. It seems as if we always want to change things about our outward appearance.

- What do you see when you look in the mirror?
- In what ways do you seek to find attention through outward appearance?

When an artist completes a piece of his art, what does he do? He admires it. He often times will stare at it, and ensure that every paint stroke, line, and color is perfect. He completes it just the way that he wants to. It is his handiwork, or masterpiece. When God created you He did the exact same thing. He admired you. He stared at you. He ensured that in everyway you were created the way that God desires you to be created. You are His masterpiece. You are His handwork. He looks at you, His creation, and smiles! The psalmist says that "He delights in you." We need to stop looking at and listening to the message of this world and begin looking at and listening to the message of the Bible! You are HIS MASTERPIECE! HE LOVES YOU!

God created you to do good works. He did not create you to do nothing, He did not create you to sit around and twirl your thumbs! This verse gives us purpose!! We have purpose because we are His, and we have purpose because God prepared and promised us good works to do!! As a follower of Jesus, we are His masterpiece-that is who we are, and our identity (His masterpiece) rolls into what we do: GOOD WORKS! Because we are God's masterpiece, He expects and prepares good works for us to do!

TODAY'S CHALLENGE
Lord, help me to see that I am your masterpiece. You created me, and you created me just the way you wanted. Help me to see that today and as a result, do good works that glorify Your Name.

Mike D'Attoma • Student Pastor • First Baptist Barnwell, SC

• DAY 23 •

O God, you are my God; earnestly I seek you; my soul thirsts for you; my flesh
faints for you, as in a dry and weary land where there is no water.
Psalm 63:1

Have you ever been so thirsty that your tongue sticks to the roof of your mouth? I am a runner and I know this feeling, it's your body's way of telling you that you need water and you need it fast.

In this Psalm we see King David crying out for God to satisfy him. David knew he needed the LORD and needed him fast. David had experienced the special presence of God before: "So I have looked upon you in your sanctuary, beholding your [God's] power and glory" (v.2). He longed to meet the LORD, blessing the name of God with his lips and lifting up his hands in praise (v.4). Have you ever felt God's special presence when you are gathered with other believers to worship? It truly is a satisfying JOY.

David knew what it was like to fellowship with God when he was all alone rather than just experiencing God in forms of corporate worship like church or student ministry. In verse 6, he makes reference to setting his mind and heart on the majesties of God in the middle of the night. Whether alone or in a group, David worshiped God because he knew that God's "steadfast love is better than life" (v. 3). Understanding this truth is what motivated David's worship for the LORD.

Does God satisfy you? Especially when you think about who God is and what He has done for you in Christ. Don't allow yourself to be caught up in everything that culture says will satisfy (money, success, relationships, reputation, etc.), instead LONG FOR GOD. Like David, the more you experience this sweet intimacy and fellowship with the LORD through a life of worship, prayer and Bible study, the more confidence you will have in the LORD to satisfy your hungering and thirsting for HIM!

TODAY'S CHALLENGE
Pray right now: Father, thank you for showing me how you are able to satisfy. Help me to hunger and thirst for you more. Increase my appetite for you and the things that please you. Help me to refuse the subtle lie of the world, that I need things my culture says will complete me. I want you to be my greatest JOY. I see that David experienced you that way and I am confident I can too. Amen.

Aaron T. Colyer • Student Pastor • MacArthur Blvd. Baptist Church, TX

• DAY 24 •

And I am sure of this, that he who began a good work in you will bring
it to completion at the day of Jesus Christ.
Philippians 1:6

With the right kind of snow, on the right kind of hill, it is super fun to start a ball rolling to create the snowball effect. You know what I mean, right? It's the kind of momentum that builds and builds until you have a massive boulder DESTROYING EVERYTHING IN ITS PATH. Maybe not that dramatic, but you get the idea.

You can see in our verse today this idea of continual growth and change when it comes to our relationship with God. He always finishes what he begins when it comes to salvation. Romans 8:29 reminds us that God is in the business of constantly conforming believers more and more into the image of Christ. This refining sanctification should give us great confidence in our relationship with God.

You see, the church at Philippi started with one man in a jail when he and his family gave their lives to Christ in a miraculous way. You should go back to Acts 16:25-34 and read it sometime. The long and the short of it is this: the man recognized his sin, turned from it, and trusted that Jesus was the only one who could pay for sin. Victory was won for him because of Christ's death and resurrection; he just finally believed!

Earlier, we established that God is in the business of finishing what he starts, but the real question is: Have you let God start that in you? Do you have a clear understanding of the gospel and have you responded to it by turning from sin and then putting your trust in Christ? If not, talk to your parents, a Christian friend, or your student pastor and ask them to help you understand the gospel from the Bible today.

If you are a Christian and find yourself struggling to walk with God, take encouragement from this verse in Philippians that God will never give up on you. He will complete the good work that he has started in you all the way until Jesus comes back! Basically you're kind of like that snowball mentioned earlier, but you have the power of the Almighty God pushing you on...

TODAY'S CHALLENGE
Pray right now: If you're not a Christian yet, cry out to God and ask for His help to bring someone to mind that you can talk with today. If you are a believer, spend some time thanking God for the fact that he will never give up on you!

Aaron T. Colyer • Student Pastor • MacArthur Blvd. Baptist Church, TX

• DAY 25 •

Therefore I tell you, do not worry about your life, what you will eat or drink; or about your body, what you will wear. Is not life more than food, and the body more than clothes?
Matthew 6:25

Worry is a powerful emotion. When we dwell on our struggles or troubles (real or perceived), we are worrying. If we are not careful these worries can even cause physical ailments. We all worry about something, however, whether it's the next text, grades, job, or even bills.

- Write down some things you are worried about in your life right now.
- Worry can be directly linked to trust. Pray over the things you wrote down and pray for greater trust in God to provide in each area.

This verse is one of my favorite all-time passages and it has greatly impacted how I live my life (and why I own 9 different colors of the exact same shirt) but I still find myself stressed out and worried at times. I mean how hard is it to not worry, especially about the basic life necessities? Isn't food and water necessary for life? If so, how can life be more than food and water?

When we live to serve Christ through sharing the Gospel and trusting Him to provide, we find that He always takes care of the necessities of life. Life fulfilled is not a life built on material possessions or earthly treasures. Worrying about wearing the hip clothes or eating at the nice restaurants won't win you any rewards. Though wanting to look your best is not wrong, clothes, food, etc. are empty, lifeless and undeserving of your worry. What if you cared about the salvation of your friends and put as much energy into leading them to Christ as you do getting new clothes, getting money to hang out friends, or getting money to buy Starbucks?

Paul says in Philippians 1:21, "For to me, to live is Christ and to die is gain." I can honestly say none of my 9, amazingly comfortable shirts will be any gain to me in life or death; in fact they are wearing out and getting old as you read this. But life, eternal life; that is what makes life worth living and it makes death and eternity in Heaven a gain. I want to encourage you not to worry about your life but instead worry about the eternal life of the lost.

TODAY'S CHALLENGE
Think of a friend or colleague who doesn't know Christ and begin to pray for their salvation. Pray for greater trust in God and His provision so that you can be focused on the eternal matters of life rather than the material things.

Chad Williams • Minister to Students & Families • Tabernacle Baptist Church, IL

• DAY 26 •

But you will receive power when the Holy Spirit comes on you; and you will be my witnesses in Jerusalem, and in all Judea and Samaria, and to the ends of the earth.
Acts 1:8

Webster's dictionary defines witness as "something serving as evidence or proof." We are that something. Our lives are serving as evidence and we are called to be a witness in our community (Jerusalem), our region (Judea), our country (Samaria), and to the world (ends of the earth).

- What is the evidence in your life to the people around you that Christ is the Messiah who died on a cross so that all might be saved?

This passage is not a request. It is a command. It is important to understand you are a witness whether you desire to be one or not. I was told once that "we are the best Christian somebody knows" which means whether you realize it or not you are what it means to be a Christian for someone. You probably don't even know they are watching but you are defining who God and Christ are in their life. When we accept Christ as savior we become a witness to God's redemptive plan and we become proof of it. So the way you interact in school with teachers and friends, at work with your boss and coworkers, at home with your family, online and elsewhere in social media speaks volumes to your view of God. Is the evidence you provide show God as powerful and capable or weak and uncaring? Maybe most importantly does your life reflect God's desire for all to be saved (John 3:17)?

You have received power for you have the Holy Spirit. It is important, therefore, that your actions represent what you believe. Do you care enough about the salvation of the lost to live out your beliefs? Will others believe God is real based on what they see in your life? There are no perfect witnesses, but as witnesses we must stand up and speak up.

TODAY'S CHALLENGE
Take a few minutes and read through the last few weeks of tweets, Facebook posts, vines, Instagram, or any other social media you may use. What do these posts reveal about what your relationship with God?

Chad Williams • Minister to Students & Families • Tabernacle Baptist Church, IL

• DAY 27 •

Walk with the wise and become wise, for a companion of fools suffers harm.
Proverbs 13:20

Most people would agree that it is important to choose our friends wisely. I can remember growing up and being heavily influenced by a group of guys I hung around. Like many young boys I wanted to be accepted by the "older" guys in my neighborhood. This led me to make some pretty foolish decisions and get into a great deal of trouble with my parents and even the police. Fortunately, God protected me from serious consequences while I was making such poor choices in friends.

- What qualities do you look for when choosing friends?
- Has there ever been a time when a friend influenced you to do something you knew was not a wise decision?

There is little doubt that we have many influences in our lives, none may be greater than the people we allow into our friend group. As a follower of Christ we have to be very careful who, we allow in our circle of influence. Relationships are at the core of who God designed us to be. And while He wants us to be engaged with those around us we have to make smart choices when deciding who our daily companions will be.

When people are allowed to enter into our lives that do not share the same Christ-centered lifestyle the influence they have can lead us from being who God desires us to be. God promises his blessing in Psalms 1:1 to those who choose their friends wisely. "Blessed is the one who does not walk in step with the wicked or stand in the way that sinners take or sit in the company of mockers".

- Are there friends that you have right now that may be influencing you to make poor decisions?
- If so, what changes do you need to make to ensure you walk wisely in the ways of the Lord?

It is important that we continually evaluate the relationships we have with others making sure that our closest companions share the same desire that we do for following the Christ.

TODAY'S CHALLENGE
Lord help me to never underestimate the power of influence people can have on my life and the power of influence I can have on theirs.

Lloyd Blank • Student Pastor • Ridgecrest Baptist Church, AL

• DAY 28 •

Now to him who is able to do immeasurably more than all we ask or
imagine, according to his power that is at work within us.
Ephesians 3:20

The imagination of a child has always been a fascinating thing. Just listen in on children playing and you will hear things like an epic battle in the Wild West as they take on a band of outlaws or Indians. There is nothing like watching a cowboy wail around on the floor after being shot with an "imaginary" arrow. Maybe it is two little girls dressed as princesses who really believe they are seated in a castle sipping tea while waiting on their carriage. Life is much simpler when we get lost in our imagination, it is in that moment that there is nothing we can't be or do. The problem is that we grow older, life gets difficult, we lose the gift of imagination that God has given us and fear keeps us from trusting that God really is able to do more than we could ever dream possible.

- What is the limit to that which you will ask God for?
- When was the last time you used your imagination and asked God for something that was well beyond your ability?

Even as followers of Christ, we often never reach our full potential in life because of the limits we put on God. Sure we include Him in our lives; asking him to bless our food, provide safe travels, help us on a test and occasionally heal the sick but that is extent of our "asking" and we almost never use our imagination when we think of what He can do. We need to understand that God says, "the sky is the limit", not to what he will do but what He can do. Ask Him anything, use your imagination, dream a big dream and you will see absolutely nothing is beyond his capability. His ability truly is beyond measure. He does not promise to give us everything we want, He just lets us know that there is nothing he is not able to do.

So with that I say ask boldly, dream big, use your imagination and do not live life with "what if". Your imagination is not bigger than God's ability, you can't ask for something God is not able to do. This is not a guarantee that you will get everything you ask for, it does teach us that God is certainly able to do more that our mind can ever conceive.

TODAY'S CHALLENGE
- Have there been times in your life that your lack of faith put limitations of what God could do? Maybe fear of failure has kept you from using your imagination to what God can do in and through you.
- Take a moment and ask God to remove the "lid" of what you have felt He was capable of doing in your life. Feel free to dream big dreams knowing He is able.

Lloyd Blank • Student Pastor • Ridgecrest Baptist Church, AL

• DAY 29 •

*Whatever you do, work at it with all your heart, as working
for the Lord, not for human masters,*
Colossians 3:23

If you are like me, we are people pleasers. We want to be liked, appreciated, and adored by other people. However, other people's opinions of us are often contingent on our performance and change with the wind. And even more than for other people, we want to do what is pleasing to us. We want to be treated fairly and we certainly do not want to do anything that seems "beneath" us. Selfishly, we do not want it to be hard, or get dirty, or sweat too much.

- What drives you when you are in class, at work, or during a game?
- Who are you trying to impress or prove something to?

Paul challenges us in this verse to view everything we do as an opportunity to serve the Lord. His use of the word "whatever" is huge because he is telling us that we do not just work with all our heart on something we enjoy doing, and we do not just work for the Lord at church or on a mission trip. Instead we view WHATEVER we are currently doing as an opportunity to "work at it with all your heart, as working for the Lord." This includes studying for a test, finishing a project, washing the dishes, the extra long practice last week, eating lunch in the cafeteria or WHATEVER you are doing.

- What are you doing right now that is hard for you to "work for the Lord?"

Doing things to seek other people's approval or acceptance and doing things to feed our own ego and ambitions gets tiring and frustrating after a while. But there is an eternal satisfaction to using your life and current circumstances for the Kingdom of God. Your schoolwork, relationships with your friends, performance on the field or in the gym, and your attitude at work are all opportunities for you to display the greatness of our Lord.

- What are you doing right now that you need to surrender to the Lord and work for Him in His freedom?

TODAY'S CHALLENGE
Lord, give me a heart to understand my current choices and circumstances are an opportunity for me to live for you. I want my life to be about you and your love for people rather than my selfish ambitions.

Jason Dorriety • Student Pastor • Spring Valley Baptist Church, SC

• DAY 30 •

If we are thrown into the blazing furnace, the God we serve is able to deliver us from it, and he will deliver us from Your Majesty's hand.
Daniel 3:17

In life, we face many peaks and valleys. Sometimes the valleys are relatively minor, like a C on a test, an argument with a friend, or a sprained ankle. Other times they are major; a failed class, the loss of a loved one, or a career-ending injury. In all of these times, our faith in the Lord is tested. Our initial response is often confusion, anger, or fear, and we pray the Lord keeps our valleys from going any deeper.

- What valleys are you facing in your life right now?
- In what circumstances are you struggling to hold on to faith in the Lord?

In this passage, Shadrach, Meshach, and Abednego were facing certain death in the fiery furnace of King Nebuchadnezzar because they had kept faith in the Lord and not bowed down to worship King Nebuchadnezzar. The valley does not get much deeper than facing death, yet these young men still had a bold faith in the Lord. They were not looking for God to keep them from the "blazing furnace," instead, they had faith He would rescue them through it.

It is so easy and natural for us to want God to keep us from the valleys, but it is often in the valleys that God demonstrates His greatness to us. He expresses His love when we feel absolutely alone. He provides His peace when nothing seems to make sense logically. He demonstrates His power when He makes a way where there seems to be no way possible. He has delivered us from the eternal "blazing furnace" through the blood of Jesus Christ on the cross. "But God demonstrates his own love for us in this: While we were still sinners, Christ died for us" (Romans 5:8).

- Do you have faith in the God who is with you in the valley, even if He doesn't keep you from the valley?

TODAY'S CHALLENGE
Read Ephesians 2:11-16.
Lord, thank You for saving me, even in my sin. When I experience the deep valleys of my life, help me hold firm to You and trust that You are working in me and walking with me through it.

Jason Dorriety • Student Pastor • Spring Valley Baptist Church, SC

• DAY 31 •

I know what it is to be in need, and I know what it is to have plenty. I have learned the secret of being content in any and every situation, whether well fed or hungry, whether living in plenty or in want.
Philippians 4:12

Imagine this... You are on your way to school, and you are confronted by a mob of students. You are beaten, hit with rocks, smacked with sticks, and even whipped. What would your reaction be?

How about this? You are on a ship headed to tell others about Jesus and the ship sinks. How would that make you feel? What if all these things don't just happen once, but over and over again? Would you be content with your life?

Paul, in the verse above, is sharing with the Philippian church that he has learned to be content whatever situation he was in. Here is a brief history of the life of Paul. He was beaten with thirty-nine lashes five times, beaten with rods three times, stoned once, shipwrecked three times, and spent a full day at sea. Yet, he was content! On his missionary journeys, he crossed dangerous rivers, went to dangerous places, was hungry, thirsty, cold, wet, and to add insult, he was imprisoned just for sharing Jesus. Yet, Paul was content. The question that comes to mind is, "what is Paul's secret to being content no matter what?" Paul found the secret in Jesus. He knew, no matter how awful the situation, Jesus was always with him, even in the bad times. He also knew that all things that happened in his life were so that he could give glory to God.

- Are you content with your life?
- What are some things you're not content with?
- How can you be content with your situation?

To find contentment you must start by giving God praise for everything in your life. Praise him for the times when life doesn't make sense. Today, you can become content by seeking God first, and knowing that even if you're persecuted, He will never leave you. So become like Paul. Be content in any and every situation whether good or bad.

TODAY'S CHALLENGE
Jesus I ask you to help me be content in every situation I find myself in today. Help me be an example to my friends and others, like Paul was to us. In Jesus name, Amen.

Greg Schmid • Teen Development Director • Bob Temple Northside Family YMCA, TN

• DAY 32 •

Do everything without grumbling or arguing.
Philippians 2:14

A recent report revealed the effects of complaining. The research showed that just half an hour per day of exposure to complaining hurts the part of the brain responsible for problem solving. In today's verse, Paul tells the church of Philippi not to complain or argue. He shares the reason why in the verses that follow; so they are blameless and pure.

Throughout the Bible there are complainers. Adam, Moses, Abraham, and David all complained about something. Think about it. Do you like to be around people that are always complaining or arguing about everything? What about you? Do your friends want to be around you? Do you complain or argue about things? So often in our lives we take things for granted, and when things don't go our way, we decide to share our complaints, even though most don't really want to be around us when we are complaining. It's pretty bad when your friends see you coming and hide (that's from personal experience). I want you to take a few minutes and think about this:

- Do your feel like you are a complainer?
- Do you argue?

If you answered yes to the questions, think about what you can do to be different. Don't be hard on yourself. We all have complained about something. Remember, God will use your situation to help others realize that complaining isn't the answer. In the meantime here are a few suggestions that may help you refrain from complaining and arguing.

- Know God has everything under control
- Set a reminder in your phone of what Philippians 4:12 says about complaining
- Be intentional and pay attention to yourself
- Realize you are not alone!

Now here is the cool part. Before today's challenge, take a moment to write down a few things that you complain about and think of ways to change the complaint into praise to God.

TODAY'S CHALLENGE
Jesus today, I want to take Philippians 2:14 to heart. I ask you to help me be an imitator of Christ and not like the world complaining about things. Turn my heart toward eternal things. I ask that You always remind me of who I am in you. Amen.

Greg Schmid • Teen Development Director • Bob Temple Northside Family YMCA, TN

• DAY 33 •

Don't let anyone look down on you because you are young, but set an example for the believers in speech, in conduct, in love, in faith and in purity.
1 Timothy 4:12

Often, the main focus of this verse for many teens is to not let anyone look down on you because you are young. Indeed, you shouldn't let others look down on you because of age. Instead, focus on what should truly be applied to your life. As a young Christian, people are watching you, especially your peers! That is why Paul says in this verse, "Teach believers (and non believers) with your life." How? You can teach others by the words you speak, the way you carry yourself, the way you treat others, the way you trust in the God you are claiming to live for, and the way you make decisions.

If you don't want anyone to look down on you because of your age, then prove you deserve respect by showing your spiritual maturity.

God wants every part of our lives. If we are to be living examples for other believers, we need to be growing in our faith. The scriptures instruct us to "come near to God and he will come near to you" (James 4:8).

Every day is a new opportunity to set an example for others. You can set an example in the classroom, on the field, in your car, at your job, and even in your house. Make the best of your opportunity today!

What are some areas in your life that you need to set an example for other believers?

TODAY'S CHALLENGE
Post this to your favorite social media account…Being young doesn't make me unable to be an example! #Growingfaith #Example #AllTimeVerses

Chase Allen • Minister to Families • Northside Baptist Church, SC

• DAY 34 •

In the same way, let your light shine before others, that they may see your
good deeds and glorify your Father in heaven.
Matthew 5:16

Whenever I am struggling to see in the dark, I turn on my handy flashlight app on my iPhone. Seriously, it's a lifesaver!

In the same way, Jesus is calling you to be like a flashlight app. As a Christ follower, you are to shine for Christ in the dark places.

Those dark places are anywhere that sin is present. It may be your school, sports team, job, circle of friends or maybe it's even your home. Obviously, this isn't always going to be easy.

When Jesus spoke again to the people, he said, "I am the light of the world. Whoever follows me will never walk in darkness, but will have the light of life."
(John 8:12)

Jesus, the light of the world, passed the torch to all Christians. We have the awesome opportunity to shine Jesus to a lost and hurting world.

Sometimes my flashlight app chooses not to work the way I want it, and at times, we choose not to shine for Christ because of the circumstances around us. It is always more important to honor God than to please man.

- Where are some places where it's easy for you to live for God?
- Has there ever been a time when you knew you needed to let your light shine, but didn't?

No matter where the darkness is, let your light shine for Jesus!

TODAY'S CHALLENGE
Father, give me strength and courage to understand that I may be the only Jesus someone ever sees. I want to shine for you in everything I do.

Chase Allen • Minister to Families • Northside Baptist Church, SC

• DAY 35 •

*Then I heard the voice of the Lord saying, "Whom shall I send? And who will
go for us?" And I said, "Here am I. Send me!"*
Isaiah 6:8

I love working with middle school students. You walk into a room and say, "I need a volunteer," and 20 hands go up! Without even being told what there are volunteering for, they are ready to do it. I wish sometimes we Christians would have that same zeal; the willingness to just do whatever is asked of us. The problem is we don't, and this is evident in many churches today. It was the same problem we read about in Isaiah 6.

In Isaiah 6, we read about Isaiah in the presence of God. He is overwhelmed not only by being face to face with God, but Isaiah recognizes his own sin. Before we can do anything for God, we must acknowledge that we are a sinner. As long as there is sin in our life, we cannot serve God completely. Once we ask Jesus to come in our lives and have that relationship God desires, then we can serve Him.

The more clearly Isaiah saw God, the more Isaiah became aware of his own powerlessness and inadequacy to do anything of lasting value without God. It is only then that God can ask the question, "Whom shall I send? And who will go for us?" It was only then that Isaiah became a willing spokesman for God when he responds "Here am I. Send me!"

- When God calls, will you say, "Here am I. Send me!"?
- Will you acknowledge that sin in your life is putting a barrier between you and God?
- Will you talk to your family and friends and tell them about Jesus?
- Will you share with your classmates and teammates about Jesus?

If God says go, will you?

TODAY'S CHALLENGE
Father, give us opportunities to share your love, grace, and mercy with those around us in our circle of influence. May we have the courage to go when You call us.

Chuck Jonas • Pastor of Worship and Students • Reidsville Baptist, GA

• DAY 36 •

But the Lord said to Samuel, "Do not consider his appearance or his height, for I have rejected him. The Lord does not look at the things people look at. People look at the outward appearance, but the Lord looks at the heart."
1 Samuel 16:7

Have you ever gone to the store around the 4th of July to buy fireworks? You're not looking for smoke bombs or sparklers. No, you want the XP-4000; the one that is supposed to shoot off 20 burst into the air! That's the one you are looking for. You find it and take it home anticipating what's going to happen when the sun goes down. You call all of your friends, and at the right time, you go outside, light the fuse, step back, and nothing happens. You're XP-4000 turns out to be a dud! It looked awesome on the outside, but didn't have what it needed on the inside.

The same thing happened to a man named Samuel. He was sent by God to anoint the next king of Israel. God told Samuel to visit a man named Jesse. One of his sons would be next king. Samuel sees Jesse's oldest son Eliab and thinks that he must be the next king. Samuel was basing his decision on appearance. That's not how God works.

God doesn't want the tallest, smartest, best looking, or most talented. Today's verse reminds us what God sees first. It's our heart He sees first and everything else comes second. Outward appearance cannot predict whether a person will faithfully obey God, because a person's actions flow from their heart. The word "heart" in scripture refers to a person's inward moral and spiritual life, including their emotions, will, and reason.

- When you see your friends, classmates, teammates, or family, are you looking at their heart or what you see on the outside?
- When people see you do they see your heart or just what's on the outside?

Continually ask the Lord to help you see the heart of others and not just their appearance or possessions.

TODAY'S CHALLENGE
Lord, help me to see the heart of those around me and not just the outside appearance.

Chuck Jonas • Pastor of Worship and Students • Reidsville Baptist, GA

• DAY 37 •

Therefore we do not lose heart. Though outwardly we are wasting away,
yet inwardly we are being renewed day by day.
2 Corinthians 4:16

Face it. Life is hard! Everyone goes through tough times. You may think your life is tough, but The Apostle Paul probably has you beat! In 2 Corinthians 11:23-28, he shares a list of hardships he faced after surrendering his life to His Lord, Jesus Christ. He tells of being beaten, stoned, whipped, shipwrecked, robbed, threatened, starved, and left for dead. Talk about a rough life! However, in today's verse Paul gives us a reason not to "lose heart" in the midst of life's trials. He reminds us even though life is hard and outwardly our bodies are wasting away, inwardly we as Christians are being renewed day by day!

Some like to think that becoming a Christian will make everything in life easier. While there may be truth to this statement, it may not be your definition of "easier." In fact, becoming a Christian can actually make your life harder because you are called to live counter to the culture. Your call to go and tell the good news, to love the unlovable, and to serve the least of these will often be met with opposition. As a Christian, you have the Holy Spirit of God dwelling within you as well as direct access to God the Father as you follow Christ's leading in your life.

When facing difficult circumstances and trials in life, remember the example of Paul. Do not lose heart. Though life may seem unbearable, remember you belong to the sovereign God of all creation. He is in control and He will see you through! Allow Christ to turn your MESS into a MESSage and your TEST into a TESTimony!

TODAY'S CHALLENGE
As you encounter challenges in life, remember the words of the hymn "Turn your Eyes upon Jesus":

"Turn your eyes upon Jesus / Look Full in His wonderful face /
and the things of Earth / will grow strangely dim /
in the light of His glory and grace!" (Helen H. Lemmel)

Ask God to teach you to trust that He is with you through every hardship, renewing you day by day!

Daniel Peavy • Student and Discipleship Pastor • First Baptist Jackson, Ga

• DAY 38 •

I can do all this through him who gives me strength.
Philippians 4:13

Who hasn't stepped up to the plate in a big game and muttered this under his breath? Have you prayed it before that big science test knowing that you failed to study? Maybe before running the mile in P.E, you quickly whispered it. Regardless of the time or reason, many people have used this verse as a source for strength and encouragement. However, what if "all this" in this verse isn't at all about sports, schoolwork, or physical endurance?

Philippians 4:13 is found within the larger text of the Apostle Paul's letter to the Christians in Philippi. Earlier in Philippians Paul explained how his imprisonment and persecution for being a follower of Christ had "actually resulted in the advance of the gospel" (Phil. 1:12). Paul continues by encouraging the Philippians to live for Christ (1:21), take on Christ's attitude (2:5-11), to be blameless and pure (2:15), to consider all else a loss compared to knowing Christ (3:7-9), and to be transformed into the likeness of Christ (3:21).

How could you live out these commands? Maybe Paul didn't understand how hard it would be to live for Christ in the 21st century. Or maybe he did? Read on to find Paul writing his concluding statements to the Christians in Philippi, "I can do ALL THIS through HIM who gives me strength!"

In reading this verse alone, you might put the emphasis on what you can do yourself. However, in understanding the context of the verse, you can see it is about what God can do in us! This verse isn't about getting an A or hitting the game winning homerun. As a Christian, you can confidently face the unknown each day, trusting that you can do anything the Lord calls you to because of his strength at work within you!

TODAY'S CHALLENGE
You are fully equipped to accomplish what the Lord has called you to accomplish. Ask Him to point out tasks he called you to do, but you failed to complete because you tried accomplishing them within your own power. Take a moment to pray; asking God to give you the mind of Christ, believing that HE can do EVERYTHING through you when HE gives you the strength to do what he has called you to do!

Daniel Peavy • Student and Discipleship Pastor • First Baptist Jackson, Ga

• DAY 39 •

But the fruit of the Spirit is love, joy, peace, forbearance, kindness, goodness,
faithfulness, gentleness and self-control. Against such things there is no law
Galatians 5.22-23

I've always loved the idea of growing my own fruit. An apple tree, pear tree, straw-berries, black berries, and raspberries have been my dream. Outside of the trees you can order from that weird "mail-order" magazine, if you plant an apple tree you typically get apples. This applies to anything you plant and this concept applies to Christians as well.

The book of Galatians is all about the effect of the Gospel in a person's life. The reality is, when a person is saved through faith in Jesus' work on the cross he or she is changed, their nature changes, their mindset changes, everything changes. We are born again the Bible says and when we are born again we now produce something, the Fruit of the Spirit.

Let's look at this in reverse. If you walk into a back yard and see apples on the ground below a tree you can deduct that it must be an apple tree. The same goes for any fruit, or nut, or veggie. Whatever fruit is produced determines what kind of tree it is. This leads to two questions we are all faced with:

- What kind of tree do you profess to be?
- What kind of tree does your life's fruit prove you are?

Many people profess to be many things, but the fruit of their life proves what they truly believe. Many people say they are a Christian but when you see how they live it doesn't match up with the picture of what we see from the Bible. I had a pastor put it this way. "Many think we come to church to get prepared for the week ahead, but what we do Monday through Saturday prepares us for worship on Sunday. On Sunday we lay at the altar of God our life that we lived the week before and say, 'here God, here is my offer of worship, my lifestyle this past week.'" What does your life's fruit say about you!

TODAY'S CHALLENGE
Lord, may we yearn to put off the fruit of the flesh that holds us down and strive to produce the fruit of the Spirit that sets us free to proclaim the gloriousness of your grace.

Jeff Walker • Pastor of Students • First Baptist Gray Gables, FL

• DAY 40 •

In the same way, faith by itself, if it is not accompanied by action, is dead.
James 2.17

Have you ever had a need for something? Maybe you needed clothes, food, or maybe money for something. Not a want, but a deep-seated need that has taken such priority in your life that it is not allowing you to function on a normal level. Now, what if when you expressed that need you were given the typical Christian cliché response of "I'll pray for you", or "may the Lord bless you", or even "go in peace, be warmed, and filled," but not actually given the needed thing. What has this response done for you?

The answer is nothing. The above is a paraphrase of James 2.14-16 that sets the context for verse 17. Read it again. What is meant by dead faith? How can faith be dead? Dead faith means worthless, unfruitful, useless, and meaningless. Dead faith does not do anything for you or those around you, as we can see from verses 14-16. James calls those with false faith self-deceived, believing they are good in God's eyes but in reality they are far from God. False faith produces boasting in one, but does not produce action towards Godly good deeds.

In Christ we are given a new nature. This new nature that we receive from God is the very thing that sets us apart from a false, dead faith. Action, works, and deeds accompany a true faith. Another way to think of this is acts of love, like Jesus said in the Sermon on the Mount, "Love God, and love your neighbor." This new nature allows us to love God and do the very things he has prepared for us to do, good deeds (Eph 2.10). In every believer is a wellspring of life (faith) that draws us to show love towards others, and this love is a picture of the Gospel.

So, what good is faith without action? About as good as telling someone who is in need of something you hope they get it! It's worthless! What is your faith today?

TODAY'S CHALLENGE
Lord, may our faith be more than intellectual; a faith whereby we experience the love you poured out on us that springs forth life and spurs us on to love and good deeds.

Jeff Walker • Pastor of Students • First Baptist Gray Gables, FL

• DAY 41 •

When you were dead in your sins and in the uncircumcision of your flesh, God made you alive with Christ. He forgave us all our sins, having canceled the charge of our legal indebtedness which stood against us and condemned us; he has taken it away, nailing it to the cross. Colossians 2:13-14

Do you know anyone who holds grudges? Someone who refuses to forgive others? Maybe that even describes you. Have you ever been wronged or hurt by someone so badly that you find it almost impossible to forgive them? Here in Colossians the Apostle Paul writes to tell us that this is not the case with God. We should be careful not to read too quickly past these verses or the truths explained here. There are two HUGE truths:

- Apart from Jesus we are spiritually dead, but Jesus died to make us alive.
- We are condemned in our sin, but Jesus took our condemnation on the cross to set us free.

We are sinners by default and without hope apart from Jesus. When we come to Jesus we are completely forgiven (Psalm 107:3). God does not hold a grudge. The forgiveness we find is not based on our own goodness or effort to be good. Instead it is based on God's unending love for us (Ephesians 2:1-10; Romans 5:8). Here is the beauty of this: you didn't do anything to earn this forgiveness, and you don't have to do anything to keep this. God doesn't look at you and see all your mistakes and failures. He isn't sitting in Heaven waiting for you to mess up. What Jesus has done on the cross is enough for you. It is enough. He loves you just as you are. No success or failure can ever change that.

- How does it make you feel to hear that God doesn't hold a grudge against you?
- Do you feel completely forgiven or are you carrying guilt?
- Have you fully placed your faith and trust in Jesus to be set free and forgiven?

TODAY'S CHALLENGE
Take a moment to write down failures and sins either from the past or that are a current struggle. Confess those things to God and ask His forgiveness for those things. Afterward, tear up the paper and throw it away. Make a list of verses that talk about God's forgiveness to look over when you are feeling guilty.

Jody Livingston • Youth Pastor • First Baptist Kennesaw, Ga

• DAY 42 •

But Daniel resolved not to defile himself with the royal food and wine, and he asked the chief official for permission not to defile himself this way.
Daniel 1:8

Ask anyone familiar with the book and life of Daniel and they will most likely tell of amazing events that occur such as Daniel in the lion's den or the fiery furnace. These were amazing for sure and most would say defining moments. However, those events would not have occurred without the decision that is recorded here in the first chapter of Daniel. This decision is truly a defining moment in the life and ministry of Daniel. It seems like a small thing and maybe even insignificant or silly for Daniel to worry about. After all, this food was from the king's table. We are not talking about happy meals or grandma's "famous" meatloaf. This was surely good food. Daniel desired holiness and obedience above all else, and for this God honored him.

- When was a time where you took a stand for your faith?
- What things make it difficult to stand up for your faith?

True defining moments in our lives are most often made when no one is around or looking. This decision of Daniel was only known by the chief official as far as we know. If we cannot stand for God and our faith in less visible moments, we will not be able to do so when everyone is looking. These defining moments that are made in secret may often feel small, insignificant, or silly. They may not always be easy to make. They may often bring challenge and may even at times be a little scary. It is crucial though for us to recognize these moments and respond in obedience in order for us to be faithful in the "bigger" moments that life will surely bring (Matthew 25:21; Luke 16:10).

- What moments in your life right now have the potential to be true defining moments?
- In what "quiet" or "secret" areas of your life is God asking for obedience?
- What things in your life are keeping you from defining moments and obedience to Jesus?

TODAY'S CHALLENGE
Lord, help me today to see and recognize the moments in my life that have the potential to be defining moments. Help me to be faithful in the things that may seem small and use me for your glory today.

Jody Livingston • Youth Pastor • First Baptist Kennesaw, Ga

• DAY 43 •

*Whatever you do, work at it with all your heart, as working
for the Lord, not for human masters*
Colossians 3:23

Before sin came to our world there was work. Did you ever think of that?

In Genesis 2:15 we see that God put man in the Garden of Eden to cultivate and keep it. This means that gathering fruit and vegetables was work, but in a good way. Imagine loving to do work! It brought Adam joy, food for life and a sense of accomplishment.

When sin came along, that same work became toilsome. In Genesis 3:17-19 God said that the ground then would produce thorns and thistles - competition for healthy plants. God also said that work then would cause us to sweat – to make us give a lot of effort.

Most people in our lifetime look at work as something that is hard and a duty they don't look forward to doing. Commercials, TV shows and movies all give work a bad name. But we should realize that God created us for work, and by realizing that is part of our human design accept work as a way of glorifying God!

When you work in retail you are serving a customer, but you are working to please God by His design. If your job is to make widgets, then make them as if God paid you. If mowing, cleaning, chores etc. are your interests then do them all to be pleasing God!

One of my favorite quotes gives a great description of what somebody looks like that loves working and is bringing glory to God.

"The master in the art of living makes little distinction between his work and his play, his labor and his leisure, his mind and his body, his information and his recreation, his love and his religion. He hardly knows which is which. He simply pursues his vision of excellence at whatever he does, leaving others to decide whether he is working or playing. To him he's always doing both." James A. Michener

---

TODAY'S CHALLENGE
Pray: God, show me how I can bring you glory with the things I consider work. Please show me what thorns and thistles are keeping me from being all I can be for You, and how to remove them from my life.

John Grigsby • Sunday School Director • Graveston Baptist Church, TN

• DAY 44 •

Then God said, "Let us make mankind in our image, in our likeness, so that they may rule over the fish in the sea and the birds in the sky, over the livestock and all the wild animals, and over all the creatures that move along the ground." So God created mankind in his own image, in the image of God he created them; male and female he created them.
Genesis 1:26-27

In Genesis 1, we see the Trinity coming together to make a decision – to create mankind. Do you ever wonder why God decided to create humans? I am a firm believer that God created us just for his joy and glory! To bring him pleasure! Like a child creating a masterpiece with watercolors and paper at the kitchen table - just painting what is fun for them … for the sheer joy of creating.

This monumental decision was made by God the Father, Son and Holy Spirit. The Trinity has been in existence since there was an existence. Imagining there was no start or end to time is a hard concept for our human minds to comprehend – but the Bible tells us it is so.

So how did God create us? What did He have in mind as a final result?
Well – Himself; a likeness of Himself. Genesis says we are created in His image and likeness.

There are at least five ways we reflect the likeness of God:

1. Love (Romans 8:38-39) – We learn true love by reflecting the example Jesus gave us.
2. Holiness (1 Peter 1:15-16) – Holy means to be separate. God is separate from us by sin, and we can separate ourselves from the world by being a part of Him.
3. Wisdom (Colossians 2:2-3) – Wisdom is deciding a course of action based upon what you know.
4. Patience (2 Peter 3:15) – Patience is to be unmoved in your posture of waiting.
5. Creativity (Genesis 2:19-20) – Man has always been creative. God gave man the first creative task by allowing Adam to create a name for each of the animals.

You were created in the image of God – embrace the multiple unique ways you are like Him!

TODAY'S CHALLENGE
Read the scripture references for each character trait. Ask God to show you the traits you need to adjust to be more like Him.

John Grigsby • Sunday School Director • Graveston Baptist Church, TN

• DAY 45 •

*Just as a body, though one, has many parts, and all its many parts
form one body, so it is with Christ.*
1 Corinthians 12:12

Go ahead and admit how much you enjoy group projects at school. It's ok; nobody has to know. Even if you are not a fan of them, you probably know how they work. The goal is to work together. If someone doesn't bring their part to the table, it can cost the entire group a good grade. Everybody is affected.

As a Christ follower, you have been given specific gifts from God. He knows you so well that he gives you exactly what he knows you can handle. You don't have to go searching for something; he gives it to you by His Spirit. You can go back and read the first eleven verses of this chapter to learn more.

Your individual preparation in God's word to seek his will for your life will lead you to group participation. You will desire to be active in the church. Just as the human body is made of many parts to allow you to live life, the church is made of many people who function as the body of Christ. Each one specifically gifted to accomplish God's mission. You are uniquely created to fit into the body of Christ. When God's people are not living out their gifts, the body of Christ is affected.

Together with other believers, you can be a part of something much bigger than yourself. When you focus on Christ and what you are to do for Him, you build up the body. How humbling to know that God has a specific plan for your life, and that you are not alone! You get to be on mission with other Christ-followers and make an impact for King Jesus.

- How well do you know where God has gifted you? Take a spiritual gifts survey.
- Are you willing to partner with other people in your church to advance the gospel to your community?
- How can you encourage unity among other Christ followers?

TODAY'S CHALLENGE
Make it a priority in the next week to reach out to an adult or senior adult in your church. Do you know their name? Their story? Get uncomfortable. Set up a lunch meeting. Watch how God uses these relationships to build unity.

Matt Sawyer • Student Pastor • Southside Baptist, AL

• DAY 46 •

I have hidden your word in my heart that I might not sin against you.
Psalm 119:11

There are over 28 million songs on iTunes. Pandora opens up a world of music by just one free app download. Hulu, Redbox, Netflix, etc. are instant gateways into endless entertainment. You could probably recite multiple song titles and their lyrics along with them. We have our favorite movie lines that we say over and over again. You may have your Call of Duty maps memorized so well that you dream you are actually in the game. That's a little extreme!

In the end do these things make a difference? Sure, we can enjoy these things, but at what cost? When do you find yourself memorizing God's word? Does music and movies take over time with God? Could they be idols?

Think about how much Scripture you could recite if you suddenly became blind and could not read God's Word. How would your spiritual life be impacted?
How much have you hidden in your heart?

Ultimately, we don't memorize scripture to get a gold star at Sunday school. God gives truth and life giving direction in his word. Not only do you become inspired inwardly when you read it, but when applied to life it reveals God's glory to a lost and dying world. Your faith grows. Your love deepens for King Jesus.
When God's word is hidden in your heart, your heart beats to please God. When difficult moments arrive you already have a plan. When temptation calls out, you know how to combat the lies. You have hidden God's word in your heart.

This is not the reality for a lot of teenagers. So many earthly things consume their minds and take over their hearts. There is a battle going on right now for your heart and mind! Even though you follow Christ, the battle gets even stronger.

Know that when you open God's word He is speaking to you. His word is active and alive.

TODAY'S CHALLENGE
Take an entertainment inventory. How much time do you spend listening to music? Watching movies? What needs to go? Purge the playlist...today. Take the challenge to memorize scripture. Find a plan that works for you. A great app to get is FighterVerses. It can be a resource to help hide God's word in your heart.

Matt Sawyer • Student Pastor • Southside Baptist, AL

*He himself bore our sins" in his body on the cross, so that we might die to sins and live
for righteousness; "by his wounds you have been healed.*
1 Peter 2:24

Stories of martyrdom litter our world don't they? A martyr is described as someone
who has died for a particular set of beliefs that they hold strongly to. Christian martyrs
gained popularity in recent history with DC Talk's book Voice of the Martyrs. In this book,
stories of modern-day martyrs are told to give us insight into the reality that people still
die for their faith in Christ today.

- Can you think of a story of a martyr in Christian history from the Bible?
- Do you know of any modern martyrs that have influenced your life?

To die a martyr's death in many cultures is an honorable thing. In fact, most people
believe that Jesus was an actual person and that he was a good man. Some may even go
to the extreme and say he died a martyr's death, dying for his belief in himself.

Peter tells us here that the death Jesus died was more than a martyr's death. He died a
substitutionary death. The words, "He himself" show us that the death of Christ was not
simply for his faith but for our redemption. Martyrs die to make a point. Jesus died to
make us clean. Jesus did not die as a martyr as some would lead us to think. He died as
a Savior.

Sacrificial living is modeled best by realizing that the death Christ died on the cross for us
is experienced by us as we come to faith in Christ. We lay our lives down and place our
faith and trust in Him alone to save us. Martyrs can't save; only sinless Saviors can. His
name is Jesus.

- Have you been crucified with Christ? How has your faith impacted you and those
  around you?
- If you have not trusted in Christ, today's challenge shares how you can.

TODAY'S CHALLENGE
Lord, I place my faith and trust in the death, burial and resurrection of Jesus as my sub-
stitute. I know that I cannot earn my salvation. My salvation has been paid for by the
blood of Jesus and I need Him to save me. Kill me and raise me again a new creation in
Christ. Amen.

Patrick Stalnaker • Pastor to Students and Families • First Baptist Kettering, OH

• DAY 48 •

For I am not ashamed of the gospel, because it is the power of God that brings salvation to everyone who believes: first to the Jew, then to the Gentile.
Romans 1:16

Shame. Many things can bring feelings of shame to our lives can't they? Like when your parents break out the videos from when you were a baby or when you are reminded of the time you did something foolish like lying to your parents, feelings of shame and guilt can rule our lives. However, feelings of shame for what we have done are not the same as being ashamed of something we have or of someone in our life.

- Can you think of a time when you were ashamed to be associated with someone?
- Has there ever been a time when you were ashamed of being a Christian?

Christians have nothing to be ashamed of. As a matter of fact, we have everything to be proud of! We have been rescued from a certain death! We have been redeemed by the God of the universe when we didn't deserve it! And we know the King! So why is it that even the Apostle Paul would write about his boldness in the face of a trip to Rome?

In Romans, Paul is sending a special letter to the church where he tells the church of his desire to come to them and preach, teach and spend time with them. He felt an obligation to preach the gospel to all people (Greeks and Non-Greeks) because He knew that the gospel proclaimed possesses the power to transform lives. He was going to the center of the known world to make known the gospel to an entirely pagan culture. He was eager to go. The need was great but the gospel was greater. The need is great today and the gospel is still greater!

- Do you wake up each day ashamed of being a Christian? Are you only a Christian around your church friends?
- How would your day be different if Romans 1:16 became a reality for you?
- Will you pray for the boldness to share your faith no matter the cost?

TODAY'S CHALLENGE
Lord, give me the boldness of Paul, through the power of your Spirit at work in me, to be bold with my faith. Help me feel the weight of the lostness in our world and a passion to impact lostness with your power-packed gospel.

Patrick Stalnaker • Pastor to Students and Families • First Baptist Kettering, OH

• DAY 49 •

Now to him who is able to do immeasurably more than all we ask or imagine,
according to his power that is at work within us
Ephesians 3:20

Maybe it's the climax of the movie, or the bottom of the ninth. Perhaps it's a breaking news story. You need to turn the volume up so that you don't miss anything. You grab the remote, and...of course! The batteries are dead! Isn't it strange how when we need the remote the most, the batteries seem to die? When we are lacking those two tiny cylinders in the remote, all the power is zapped away. It's nothing more than a cheap plastic case with buttons.

Far too often, Christians rely on their own power in life. This "power" seems dead, like we are trying to operate with no batteries. Our own power says "pick yourself up by your bootstraps." The gospel, however, says to be daily dependent upon the power of Jesus. In Ephesians 3:20, Paul reminds us that there is an infinitely greater power that we have access to than our weak personal batteries. We have a power in Christ that is able to do "far more abundantly than all that we ask or think, according to the power at work within us."

Paul is saying that in that difficult relationship you are facing, Christ gives the power to forgive and love. In the face of fear, Christ gives the power of trust. In the depths of doubt, Christ gives the power of hope. We don't conjure up our own power; it's granted to us richly through the gospel. And this isn't AAA battery power; no, it's the universe-forming, cosmic-shaking power that Christ has had since eternity past and will have forever. It is big time spiritual power. And in the gospel, it flows freely out of his grace. So ask for it, accept it, and thank him for it. He loves lavishing his children with gospel power for the glory of his holy name.

TODAY'S CHALLENGE
Jesus, your name alone is great and powerful. In my weakness, your power is made all the more glorious. I have doubts and fears, but your resurrection power reminds me of the hope in your name. Empower me today to live by your power, to love by your power, and to serve by your power.

Jesse Payne • Student Pastor • Lakeland Baptist Church, TX

• DAY 50 •

Therefore, there is now no condemnation for those who are in Christ Jesus
Romans 8:1

Growing up, some things were crystal clear to me. When my coach yelled my number, it was crystal clear that I needed to listen up. When my mom said my full name, it was crystal clear that I was in trouble. When my parents cheered at my games, it was crystal clear that they loved and supported me. I didn't have to wonder about my standing in these situations; I knew exactly what these people meant. Their thoughts were crystal clear.

It's easy to forget about the crystal clear words of God. God has called you "chosen, holy, and dearly loved." He's called you "child." He's called you "pure." And in Romans 8:1, he has told you that for those in Christ, there is no condemnation. None. Guilt and punishment no longer exists for those in Christ. He is crystal clear in his love and grace toward undeserving sinners.

The beauty of the gospel is that when God looks at someone in Christ, he sees them clothed in the perfect righteousness of His Son. He sees a beloved child. He sees a beautiful spotless member of the family of God. There is no wrath toward them, no condemnation. They are free, loved, pure, saved, and secure. He holds no love back, because he holds no condemnation toward them. The cross absorbed his wrath, and we now walk in grace.

Jesus doesn't have a list of your sins in his back pocket. He doesn't shake his head in disappointment. Jesus doesn't roll his eyes when you fail. Jesus doesn't sulk in shame. He loves you and empowers you and strengthens you and cares for you. He has been crystal clear about how he feels about you, right now, today, where you are. "No condemnation."

TODAY'S CHALLENGE
Jesus, thank you that you don't keep a notebook of my wrongs. Thank you for forgiving them all upon the cross; once and for all. Remind me of your full-throttle grace toward me every day. Help me to walk in freedom, free of guilt and condemnation. And help me to have this same spirit of grace towards others, just as you have had toward me.

Jesse Payne • Student Pastor • Lakeland Baptist Church, TX

• DAY 51 •

Do not merely listen to the word, and so deceive yourselves. Do what it says.
James 1:22

Often times after delivering a sermon or finishing a youth talk I will have someone come up and tell me how much they enjoyed the talk. Then less than ten minutes later the person is living totally opposite of what we just read in Scripture and talked about. While hearing the message of the Word is important, acting in obedience to the Word is paramount.

With this verse James begins to explain that hearing without doing is a self-deception. This may be considered one of the major themes of the letter. The thought is strikingly similar to that of Rom 2:13, where both "hearers" and "doers" appear. James goes on to caution his readers not to remain hearers only. The word "hearers" is used in the New Testament only in this context and in Romans 2:13. It suggests hearing the public reading of Scriptures, but in the present context it obviously refers to hearing the gospel message. The author is saying that merely hearing, or even knowing, the message is not enough. What really counts is putting into practice what you hear and know, that is, to live out the gospel message, transforming it into action.

I can tell you that I am a star baseball player (if you saw me you would chuckle right now!). However, unless I am able to do the things A-Rod or Cal Ripkin can do on the field then I am probably deceiving you and myself. It is the same way with obedience to the Word of God. As we listen and apply it to our life we should be called to action.
Christ gave us many opportunities to hear the message and respond in obedience. We are to love our neighbors. We are to tell others about the Gospel message that changed our life. We are to trust God with ALL of our life.

TODAY'S CHALLENGE
Hear God speak action into your life, then act on it. Be Jesus to the World.

David Richardson • Associate Pastor Youth/Missions • First Baptist Creedmoor, NC

• DAY 52 •

If my people, who are called by my name, will humble themselves and pray and seek my face and turn from their wicked ways, then I will hear from heaven, and I will forgive their sin and will heal their land.
2 Chronicles 7:14

Do you remember learning about "If-Then Statements" in math class? Here's a memory jog...."If-then statement is a conditional statement in the form 'If A, then B, where A is a hypothesis and B is a conclusion.' An if-then statement is used in deductive reasoning." Does your head hurt yet? Our scripture reference today is an "if-then statement" between the great King Solomon and the Lord.

In 2nd Chronicles 6, Solomon has just finished building God's temple. Solomon gave God the glory for all of the blessings Israel was enjoying. When the nation of Israel made the Lord their sole object of worship, He blessed them. Yet, Solomon knew the history of God's people. They had come to a place of prosperity and peace before (see the book of Joshua), only to fall away from the Lord repeatedly (see Judges and beyond). Knowing this history, Solomon prefaced his dedication prayer with asking God to remember Israel's faithfulness if they were to fall away. God answers with an "if-then statement".

In 2nd Chronicles 7:12-14, God responds,"Then the Lord appeared to Solomon by night, and said to him: "I have heard your prayer, and have chosen this place for Myself as a house of sacrifice. When I shut up heaven and there is no rain, or command the locusts to devour the land, or send pestilence among My people, if My people who are called by My name will humble themselves, and pray and seek My face, and turn from their wicked ways, then I will hear from heaven, and will forgive their sin and heal their land.'"

This same "if-then statement" is available to America. The choices our country has made over the last two centuries has led us to turn our backs on God in the home, classroom, courts and even in some churches. However, our generation...your generation can help us complete this equation. IF we put politics aside and sincerely turn back to the ways of following God by humbling ourselves and seeking the face (and will of God), He will THEN hear us and we will be forgiven and healed.

TODAY'S CHALLENGE
#IFTHEN – IF we pray, seek, turn, THEN God hears, heals and forgives

David Richardson • Associate Pastor Youth/Missions • First Baptist Creedmoor, NC

• DAY 53 •

Children, obey your parents in the Lord, for this is right.
Ephesians 6:1

Have you ever been in a grocery store and noticed the children who stand in line at the register and just gaze upon the candy? Not only do they gaze upon the candy, they touch, pick up, put on the conveyor, open the package, all while their parent or guardian is saying "No, put that back," or "If you don't listen..." or the best, when the middle name is yelled. If the child would only obey their parent, all of the embarrassment for everyone would be nonexistent. All young children, at times, disobey and test their parent's limits.

- When was the last time you tested your parent's limits?
- Why do you think that the Bible teaches to obey your parents?

When you are walking with Jesus in your daily life, obeying your parents will be one of the many things that will come easy. The word for obey is different from the term submission. Obedience involves recognition of authority.

- Is it difficult for you to recognize your parents as the authority in your life?
- Is your relationship with God where it needs to be?

In obedience to your parents, you are not only recognizing their authority in your life, but you are also recognizing God's authority. God designed for his people to have firm relationships with one another where respect, submission, obedience, and love are evident. If you want peace at home with your parents, you must first be obedient to God. Once your relationship with God is right, the rest will be an overflow of what He is doing in your life.

Be in constant obedience with God, so that your earthly relationships will be full of abundance!

TODAY'S CHALLENGE
Pray for your parents. They are making decisions for you and your family. Ask God to grant them wisdom and peace as they lead your family.

Ryan West • Student Pastor • FBC McGehee, AR

• DAY 54 •

Avoid godless chatter, because those who indulge in it will
become more and more ungodly.
2 Timothy 2:16

Think back to your time in kindergarten when there was someone who said something mean to you. You might have replied with "Sticks and stones may break my bones, but words will never hurt me." While as a child that seemed to be a good comment, you may realize now that words actually do hurt you. The words that you speak hold great weight! Think about when someone says something positive to you or about you. It makes you feel good. You like to hear people say good things about you!

- When was the last time you said something positive to someone?
- Do you find yourself saying hurtful things to people?

If you are going to become more like Christ, it is important to talk like Christ. Avoiding godless chatter is one way that you can be more like Jesus. All throughout Scripture, you never see Jesus in a group talking bad about people. Jesus spoke with kindness, and was looking to encourage others. When we indulge in godless chatter, it does more than just come out in words. The things that we hear and talk about, often lead to us acting upon these things. Avoiding the negative talk, the negative music, the negative television shows, will have an overall impact on your life. Striving to be more like Jesus should be our goal; so therefore, we must avoid the negative influences in our life to the best of our ability. Speak positive words. Listen to positive music. Surround yourself with things of God, and not of this world!

TODAY'S CHALLENGE
Strive to speak positive words to those around you! If your friends begin to talk about someone, leave the conversation, or add a positive remark about the situation.

Ryan West • Student Pastor • FBC McGehee, AR

• DAY 55 •

Therefore, since we are surrounded by such a great cloud of witnesses, let us throw off everything that hinders and the sin that so easily entangles. And let us run with perseverance the race marked out for us, ²fixing our eyes on Jesus, the pioneer and perfector of faith. For the joy set before him he endured the cross, scorning its shame, and sat down at the right hand of the throne of God.
Hebrews 12:1-2

When you read the above text underline the phrase "run with perseverance." Life is a struggle isn't it? We have deadlines, meetings, tests, family, and countless other demands. Each day we wake up, life seems to get more hectic. The writer of Hebrews is reminding his readers to keep going and not give up in the spiritual race they are running. There are days we want to quit. There are moments we want to stop and throw in the towel. How do we "run with perseverance" each day of our lives? The writer gives us three ways to run with endurance in this passage.

First, he says to listen to the witnesses. He spends all of chapter eleven reminding readers of people all throughout the Old Testament who have gone before them. People like Noah, Abraham, Moses, and Rahab. He lists men and women who did not give up in the face of adversity and conflict. Allow their testimony and faithfulness to encourage you as we run this gospel race.

Second, he says to cast off the heavy weight. The writer tells these readers to run with perseverance by removing the heavy weights. Running with perseverance is difficult when we are weighted down. He mentions to throw off everything that hinders, specifically the sin that easily entangles us. We all struggle with certain sins and, if left alone, find ourselves entangled by sin. Perhaps it is the sin of anger, lust, jealousy, greed, or malice. As long as we allow ourselves to be weighted down with sin, we will find it very difficult to run with endurance.

Finally, he says to focus on Christ. The writer reminds the readers to fix their eyes on Christ, the author and perfector of their faith. Christ endured the cross, shunned the shame, and is now seated at the right hand of God the Father. Christ is the one who our eyes are to be fixed on as we run this race with endurance. We are not to fix our eyes on our troubles, our afflictions, or other people. We are to fix our eyes on Christ.

TODAY'S CHALLENGE
As you run this gospel race recall, those who have gone before you, confess the sins that are weighing you down, and place your eyes squarely on Christ your Redeemer and Savior.

David O'Dell • Pastor • Hardy Street Baptist, MS

• DAY 56 •

Because the Lord disciplines the one he loves, and he chastens
everyone he accepts as his son.
Hebrews 12:6

What thoughts come to your mind when you hear the word "discipline"? You might think of sitting in time out, or being grounded, or having your phone taken from you. I imagine all kinds of pictures come to your mind when you think of someone being disciplined.

This verse in Hebrews is a quote from Proverbs 3:11-12. The implication in Proverbs and in Hebrews is a father talking with a son. I am a father of four children, and part of my responsibility as a parent to my children is to discipline them as they grow up. I have been given the responsibility by God to ensure they grow in a godly manner. But what does the writer of Hebrews have in mind when he uses the word discipline in this passage?

Take a moment and read Hebrews 12:4-11, and circle each time you read the word discipline. The word is used nine times in these eight verses. I want you to understand what this word originally meant in order to better understand what the writer here is telling the readers. The word that he uses here means, "to provide instruction for informed and responsible living, educate "or "to assist in the development of a person's ability to make appropriate choices, practice discipline." A better word used here would be to train instead of discipline.

Go back and read Hebrews 12:4-11 and read the word train each time you see the word discipline. Makes more sense right? You see, there are times in our lives when we go through difficult hours in which we know God is not disciplining or punishing. Rather we are going through training in order to run the race with endurance. God is working our faith muscles to better prepare us for the gospel race we living. There are periods of your life where God is strengthening you in order to prepare you to run your gospel journey.

In this verse the writer says God disciplines those whom He loves. You see, if God did not love you he would not discipline or train you. It is in His love for you where you will find His heart to train you for greatness. What is an area of your life in which God is training you?

TODAY'S CHALLENGE
Pause and ask the Lord to show you the areas he is trying to train you in order to better prepare you for the race that lies ahead of you.

David O'Dell • Pastor • Hardy Street Baptist, MS

• DAY 57 •

All Scripture is God-breathed and is useful for teaching, rebuking,
correcting and training in righteousness,
2 Timothy 3:16

Do you remember the Swiss Army Knife? They are still popular today. The Swiss Army Knife was not your ordinary knife. It was more than a knife. It had all these extras to help a person survive. I can remember as a kid when I saw my first Swiss Army Knife. All the boys in my neighborhood had Swiss Army Knives. As a boy, you had to have one. If we went into the woods, you always took your Swiss Army Knife. The Swiss Army Knife made us feel like we had everything we needed to survive in the woods.

In 2 Timothy 3:16, God tells us that the Bible is like a Swiss Army Knife. The Bible is a must for the Christ-follower. We cannot live without it. The Bible gives the Christ-follower everything he needs to survive in our world today. The Apostle Paul tells us that the Bible is God-breathed or inspired. In other words, God inspired the authors of the Bible through the Holy Spirit to write the Word of God (see 2 Peter 1:20-21). The Bible is the very Word of God. It is our source of truth. God gave us the Bible to help us to live a godly life through Christ Jesus.

The Bible has many uses like the Swiss Army Knife. It is useful to show what is right (teaching). It is useful to show us what is not right (rebuking) and to correct us when we do what is wrong (correcting). Lastly, the Bible is useful to train us to stay right with God (training). The Bible is essential for the Christ-follower. God has given us the Bible to help us live a Christ-honoring life in our world today.

TODAY'S CHALLENGE
Lord, help me to see how much I need the Bible in my life. Give me a hunger for the Bible where I cannot live without it on a daily basis.

Shane Newton • Student Pastor • Southside Baptist Church, AL

• DAY 58 •

Therefore, as God's chosen people, holy and dearly loved, clothe yourselves with compassion, kindness, humility, gentleness and patience.
Colossians 3:12

A little girl was on the way home from church when she turned to her mother and said, "Mommy, the preacher's sermon this morning confused me."

The mother asked, "Why is that?" The girl replied, "Well, he said that God is bigger than we are. Is that true?"
"Yes, that's true," the mother replied. "He also said that God lives within us. Is that true, too?" Again the mother replied, "Yes."
"Well," said the girl, "If God is bigger than us and He lives in us, wouldn't He show through?"

Colossians 3:12 reminds us of what should be seen in a Christ-follower's life. We should have characteristics that our Lord Jesus had. Colossian 3:5-9 shows us characteristics we shouldn't have. Characteristics like sexual immorality, lust, idolatry, anger, filthy language, and lying should not be seen in believers. Our key verse says, "as God's chosen people," meaning that we have a new life in Christ. Our old self has died and we have a new life in Christ.

Paul paints a picture in these verses of taking off the old clothes and putting new clothes on. God's people will take off the old clothes and put on the new clothes that identify them with Christ. Jesus showed compassion, kindness, humility, gentleness, and patience. As a Christ-follower, those same characteristics should be seen in our life.

This year our student ministry attended the Almighty Mud Run. The Mud Run is a 5k run with 25 obstacles. We started the run with our nice, clean clothes. We finished the run with smelly, filthy clothes. After the race, the clothes were taken off and thrown away. Any characteristics that are not pleasing to God need to be taken off. Get rid of them and put on Christ.

As the little girl asked, "If God is bigger than us and He lives in us, shouldn't he show through our lives?" He should be showing through. People should see Christ living through us. They should see characteristics of compassion, kindness, humility, gentleness, and patience.

TODAY'S CHALLENGE
Lord, show me if there are any characteristics that I need to get rid of. Help me be like Christ so that others see Christ in me.

Shane Newton • Student Pastor • Southside Baptist Church, AL

• DAY 59 •

Hear, O Israel: The Lord our God, the Lord is one. Love the Lord your God with all your heart and with all your soul and with all your strength.
Deuteronomy 6:4-5

---

iPhone, iPad, Android, Instagram, Twitter, Facebook, a video game, a sport, band, choir, hanging out with friends... How many hours a day do you spend doing these things? None of these are evil, but each of them have the ability to take too much of your time. They can distract you from having a real and lasting relationship with the one and only true Lord.

- What takes up the most of your time each day?
- How much time do you spend with Jesus?

In this passage, the Israelites were getting ready to go into the Promised Land. God wanted to make sure that their focus was on Him because they could be so easily distracted. If God could sum up everything He wanted them to do in one sentence, it would be this: "Love the Lord your God with all your heart and with all your soul and with all your strength." You can break that down by simply saying, "Love God with every breath." Every breath that you take, you can love God more than the breath before.

God promised to give the Israelites a certain piece of land flowing with milk and honey. He said that He would take care of all their needs. He's done so much more for you. He has given you everlasting life and the forgiveness of your sins through His Son, Jesus Christ! Every breath you take should praise His name!

It is so easy to fill time with everything this world has to offer. God deserves all of you... your heart... your soul... and your strength. He is the one and only true Lord. Love God with every breath.

How can you show God that you love Him with every breath?

TODAY'S CHALLENGE
Lord, you are more important to me than anything else in my life. I will choose to love you with all my heart, my soul, and my strength. I love you with every breath.

Jay Smith • Associate Pastor of Youth & Education • Screven Baptist Church, SC

• DAY 60 •

*For it is by grace you have been saved, through faith—and this is not from yourselves, it
is the gift of God—not by works, so that no one can boast.*
Galatians 2:8-9

Who wants to be made right with God and go to heaven? It's not that hard, but you
have to do everything in the right order and for the exact amount of time. Here are the
rules... Ready... Set... Go! Do 10 jumping jacks while holding your breath, spin around 15
times to the right then 7 times to the left, (you can start breathing again), run exactly 30
feet as fast as you can then do the "worm" on the ground for a solid minute. Get up and
begin acting like a chicken while bobbing for apples, (you must collect 3 apples within
20 seconds), then stand on your head without falling over for 2 minutes. Once you've
completed that, then... ok, so that's not how you make things right with God. As a matter
of fact, you can't actually "do" anything.

Focus on these two truths:

1. Grace is a gift that you don't deserve. Just one "tiny" sin that you have committed
    has separated you for eternity from a holy and righteous God. He is perfect and
    you cannot even stand in His presence. According to Galatians 2:12, mankind
    was considered aliens and strangers to God without any hope. Grace is unde-
    served favor. Jesus Christ gave up His life for you so that you could be made right
    with God.

2. Faith is you believing in what Christ has already done for you. To be saved, you
    need to have faith that Jesus Christ came in the form of man, died for your sins,
    and rose again the third day. Note: you didn't have to do anything. You were
    incapable of saving yourself. You needed God to do it for you... and He did!

Selfishness is at the root of every sin. People become selfish even concerning salvation.
Remember, God died for you. How will you live for Him today?

TODAY'S CHALLENGE
Father, thank You for sending Your son to die in my place. I could not gain salvation on my
own. I humbly bow in Your presence and ask You to use me for Your glory. My salvation
is by grace through faith in Jesus Christ alone.

Jay Smith • Associate Pastor of Youth & Education • Screven Baptist Church, SC

• DAY 61 •

Then Jesus declared, "I am the bread of life. Whoever comes to me will never go hungry, and whoever believes in me will never be thirsty."
John 6:35

They were the best I'd ever had and twelve years later, I still haven't found any tacos that compare. I was an exchange student in Mexico City when I discovered tacos al pastor from a roadside restaurant. The flame kissed pork, homemade tortillas, and fresh pico de gallo...oh, how I'd love to make it back there some day! Perhaps you have a favorite dish. Most of us do. Maybe it's something that reminds you of the holidays or from your favorite restaurant. Interestingly, no matter how many times we satisfy that longing, we still find ourselves wanting more. We can't wait until we can eat it again.

The longing for food is but one of our physical longings. Just as we experience hunger, we also thirst, have a desire for comfort, etc. I believe these physical pangs help us understand a deeper set of longings, those of the spirit. We long for peace, hope, love, and righteousness. But how do we fulfill these spiritual longings?

As Jesus fed the 5,000, He satisfied the physical hunger of the people, but their hunger returned the next day. Jesus then pointed them to a deeper, spiritual longing. He claimed to be the "Bread of Life" that would forever fulfill them. If they would eat of the Bread of Life, they would never hunger again.

While he could provide them with food for their stomachs, His purpose was to satisfy that deep sense of hunger within their spirits. He serves the same purpose today. He gives us peace and hope. He shows us love and clothes us in righteousness. He wants to fill your hungering spirit. He is the Bread of Life that has come from heaven, and He is the only one that can satisfy you. Do you know Jesus in this way? Let Him fill you and you will never hunger again. "Blessed are those who hunger and thirst for righteousness, for they will be filled."

TODAY'S CHALLENGE
Father, sometimes my spirit hungers and thirsts and I cannot satisfy this longing on my own. Let me find fulfillment in Jesus. Amen.

B.J. Cobb • Associate Pastor • Northside Baptist Church, GA

• DAY 62 •

When Jesus spoke again to the people, he said, "I am the light of the world. Whoever follows me will never walk in darkness, but will have the light of life."
John 8:12

Once upon a time...you can probably fill in the rest. While the characters are interchangeable, generally speaking, fairy tales are all the same. There may be a princess, knight, stepmother, godmother, hobbit, dwarf, or droid. There's always a villain and a hero representing good and evil, respectively. In fairy tales, evil is depicted as dark, cold, and shadowy. Good shows up as radiant, vibrant, and colorful.

But regardless of the various personas, the storylines follow a fairly predictable pattern. "Character-A" has a chance at something great but faces seemingly insurmountable circumstances. The situation is elevated whenever the villain tries to stop "A." Just when it appears that all hope is lost, the hero enters and saves the day. The princess finds true love. The ring is destroyed. The empire is restored. Evil is defeated and good is triumphant.

I believe we connect so well with fairy tales, because they hint at something that is real and true about our world. In the great story of God, Satan is the villain, Christ, the hero. You and I, and everyone who has come before and all those who will come after us, are those in desperate need of help. Our situation is hopeless. We've all sinned and thereby earned death.

But in our darkest moment, the hero has something to say. Jesus proclaimed to be the "light of the world." That's good news for you and me. Just as good defeats evil, light overcomes darkness. Jesus, the light, pushes back evil and darkness. He wins! Satan loses. But we have a response. We must follow him so that we do not walk in darkness. When it's dark, we stumble and sometimes fall. We must commit to walking in the light, as He is in the light.

TODAY'S CHALLENGE
Allow the Light of the World to enter your life, illuminate your sin, and push back the darkness within. And then, walk in that Light.

B.J. Cobb • Associate Pastor • Northside Baptist Church, GA

• DAY 63 •

Therefore confess your sins to each other and pray for each other so that you may be healed. The prayer of a righteous person is powerful and effective.
James 5:16

Society today teaches that you must always "have it together." No one could love you "as you really are," so you must hide all your flaws so that you can be accepted. As the great philosopher, Fergie, put it, "Big girls (and especially boys) don't cry!" The result in our churches is shallow relationships where you can know somebody for years without understanding a single meaningful thing about them.

- When this week have you felt pressure to hide who you are from the world?

The Gospel, however, could not be more different than the teaching of this world. Christ is intimately aware of everything about us. The message of the cross is that there is literally no sin within us that is hidden from God, yet despite our brokenness, because of his great love for us, he sent his son to die in our place. Let that sink in!

- If God can love you, despite your mistakes, what does that say about how you, being his child, should respond to the sin of others?

When you cannot be real about your sin with another trusted believer, you miss out on their prayers (which are powerful and effective) and something else that is crucial to your growth... accountability. By the way, the person who holds you accountable should be older, or at least more spiritually mature than you. As Paul was to Timothy, Elijah was to Elisha, Moses was to Joshua, and Jesus was to the disciples, you need an older believer investing in your life. And yes, parents can make some of the best accountability partners. Is that hard to swallow? Well, if you truly hate your sin, you will take steps to make sure that sin is removed despite your discomfort, and no one loves you and is more invested in your life than mom and dad.

TODAY'S CHALLENGE
Father, help me be courageous and intentional today about finding someone who can hold me accountable for the sin in my life.

Alan Ostrzycki • Student Pastor (Children/Jr. High) • Lindsay Lane Baptist Church, AL

• DAY 64 •

No temptation has overtaken you except what is common to mankind. And God is faithful; he will not let you be tempted beyond what you can bear. But when you are tempted, he will also provide a way out so that you can endure it.
1 Corinthians 10:13

Growing up, I can remember when WWJD bracelets first hit the market. An idea that started in one guy's garage became a "Christian sensation" overnight. Although, the movement has lost some steam over the years, some of you reading this may have one on your wrist right now. Apart from the obvious fashion statement or serving as an evangelistic tool, I question the idea behind these bracelets.

If you ever find yourself in a situation in which you have to look down at your wrist and ask yourself, "Would Jesus do what I am about to do?" the answer is obvious… "NO!" In my day, with "True Love Waits" rallies every other weekend, the common question raised by teens was, "How far is too far?" What they mean is "How close can I get to sin before it is actually sin?"

That question is like a soldier in battle asking, "How close can I get to this guy with a flamethrower before I am completely engulfed in flames?" Do you get my point? As a child of God, you must quit playing with sin because your enemy is not! Maybe the reason you still struggle with sin in your life is because you keep that sin at arm's reach when Christ has called you to "flee all appearances of evil (1 Thessalonians 5:22)." God is very clear. The way to stand up under temptation is simple… Run from it as fast as you can! God has given you a way of escape.

- Is there a sin in your life that you need to escape from? Confess that sin to Christ today.
- What behaviors/friends/situations do you need to avoid in order to escape that sin?

TODAY'S CHALLENGE
God, help me not only to identify sin in my life, but to run from any opportunity to sin today.

Alan Ostrzycki • Student Pastor (Children/Jr. High) • Lindsay Lane Baptist Church, AL

• DAY 65 •

Flee the evil desires of youth and pursue righteousness, faith, love and peace, along with those who call on the Lord out of a pure heart.
2 Timothy 2:22

Have you ever seen a little dog that will bark at you and look fierce and then when you take a step towards it, it will run for its life? When I think of the word "flee," that is the image that I get: running for your life. Yet when we read these words from 2 Timothy 2:22, I don't think we understand just how much God wants us to run from sin. Flee! Run as if your life depended on it. In the same verse we see the opposite illustration. Pursue. I am not sure you could find a clearer picture of the things that we are to run toward - righteousness, faith, love and peace; all good things. It isn't a spiritual game where we go back and forth, it is meant to urge us as we grow up and mature to run from bad things and chase after the things of God. Be about His work and not of our own.

- Has there been a time when you have found yourself embracing temptation instead of running from it?
- In order to pursue righteousness, what are some things you need to leave behind?

We need to daily pray for a pure heart, the heart of God. Choosing to do the right thing is sometimes difficult and not without heartache. But God uses his people who avoid their youthful desires and a pure heart to do His good work. Paul is giving Timothy much-needed advice on how to deal with problems in the local church. He is passionate about moving towards the things of God; not just in a laid-back fashion, but hot pursuit! Run towards God with a pure heart.

TODAY'S CHALLENGE
Run! Run after righteousness, faith, love and peace and you will be fleeing from sin at the same time! Look for opportunities today to put a pure heart into action.

Dustin Sams • Student Pastor • Second Baptist Church, AR

• DAY 66 •

Therefore, if anyone is in Christ, the new creation has come:
The old has gone, the new is here!
2 Corinthians 5:17

"Watch where you are going!"

What a great phrase and some very sound advice. Most of the time we hear it when we are doing exactly the opposite. It usually leads to us paying attention, at least for a time. There is a good reason that the driver's seat in a vehicle is facing towards the front. It would be virtually impossible to safely get to your destination while facing down the road that you have already traveled. We are supposed to check our rearview mirrors, not stare into them as we drive forward. But some of us live our lives doing just that: focusing on reliving the past while we stumble into the future.

The apostle Paul tells us that in Christ the old has gone, the new is here! When we put on the salvation of Christ, that old person is gone, the new person is here. Be encouraged about your future in Christ; be done with spending time dwelling on past failures.

- Are there things from your past causing heartache today?
- Do you struggle with shame or forgiving yourself?

If you are in Christ, you are a new creation! Let that sink in a little bit. You don't have to let your history define your future. History can be just that: history. God is faithful to forgive our sins. All we have to do is ask. Isn't that great?

But that is just part of it. We also must forgive ourselves and move forward. Guilt and shame from things for which we have already asked God to forgive us prevents us from becoming all that God has planned for us to be. Keep moving forward, looking ahead, and living every day as God's new creation!

TODAY'S CHALLENGE
Embrace God's new creation in you and remember to rejoice in the person you are and who you are becoming in Christ. Your past doesn't have to determine your future.

Dustin Sams • Student Pastor • Second Baptist Church, AR

• DAY 67 •

This is how we know what love is: Jesus Christ laid down his life for us.
And we ought to lay down our lives for our brothers and sisters.
1 John 3:16

"All You Need Is Love" is an epic song written in the late 60's that you would recognize if you heard it! The band that recorded and performed this iconic song was none other than The Beatles (arguably the greatest band of all time). The Beatles were commissioned to write a song for the United Kingdom's portion of a global television event where millions of people would be watching. After the event, the song quickly topped the charts in multiple countries for weeks. The song united people around the world and gave them a common message that love is the most important thing in life and is really all you need.

What a powerful message for the world to hear. However, the questions that we are left with answering ourselves are crucial.

- What does real love actually look like when lived out?

The apostle John wrote 1 John as a way of reassuring believers in their faith and sharing his first hand experience with Jesus. He saw and felt what true love was all about when he watched the son of God give his life for humanity on a cross.

This world is filled with "Lovestitutes"! (substitutes for real love) We see "lovestitutes" on TV with shows, movies, at school and maybe even at home. "Lovestitutes" are fake and give the illusion of love through intense emotion. However, real love is sacrificial, giving, and selfless. When we lay down our lives for our brothers and sisters, we reflect Jesus' love when he sacrificed himself for us. Showing real love is putting others before yourself or giving up something you care about for someone else to benefit. Real love inevitably points others to Jesus. Jesus calls us to love our neighbor as we would love ourselves which is not an easy thing to do.

- What ways can you start to show the people in your life real love?
- Love is something that can unify people. Real love is something that can change people's lives.

TODAY'S CHALLENGE
God, thank you for showing me what real love truly is. I want opportunities to share real love with others, help me make the most of those opportunities and for those people to see Jesus through it.

Kent Bjurstrom • Pastor of Student Ministries • Sugar Grove Church, IN

• DAY 68 •

Calling his disciples to him", Jesus said, "Truly I tell you, this poor widow has put more into the treasury than all the others. They all gave out of their wealth; but she, out of her poverty, put in everything—all she had to live on.
Mark 12:43-44

There may be nothing quite as entertaining as a high school basketball game between two great teams on a Friday night. On the court, the most athletic gets all the publicity, the college scholarships and the fame. There was a particular high school team that was loaded with talent. There was one student on that team that sat at the end of the bench. He never had a bad attitude about playing time, or about the awards that never came his way. He was just happy to give everything he could. One day near the end of the season, someone wanted to speak with him. No one ever wanted to talk to him about his season. An elderly gentleman approached him and told him that his attitude about the game of basketball, the type of teammate he was and the way he maximized his talent was inspiring. This gentleman told him he had a full ride scholarship to the college of his choice because of what he saw in him. This high school student gave absolutely everything he had to his team, even though to many it didn't seem like much.

From a very early age, we are taught by society, media and people that bigger is always better. Bigger bank accounts, better cars, bigger boats, bigger houses, bigger cell phones, bigger quantities of food and full closets are what we are conditioned to think about. Jesus takes a different stance. In the midst of rich people throwing sacks of money in an offering box, a poor widow enters and gives absolutely everything. It pales in comparison to the amount given by those before her. In spite of that fact, Jesus tells his disciples that she gave more than all the others because she gave everything.

The heart behind the gift is what Jesus was after. The woman gave pennies but it was all she had She wanted God to have everything. Jesus wants all of who you are. Are you giving a portion of who you are to Jesus or everything?

TODAY'S CHALLENGE
Create a list of all the things that keep you from giving God everything. Hang that list in a place you will see it regularly, to remind you of the things that are holding you back. Work on eliminating those things so God can use more than just the portion you are giving Him.

Kent Bjurstrom • Pastor of Student Ministries • Sugar Grove Church, IN

• DAY 69 •

The thief comes only to steal and kill and destroy; I have come that
they may have life, and have it to the full.
John 10:10

There is a thought that we must realize as Christians. Satan wants to destroy our lives. He does not want us to be happy. In fact, it is quite the opposite. He wants our lives to be miserable. He will do anything he can to steal, kill and destroy your walk with Christ.

However, there is another thought we must realize: Jesus came to give us life. He came to give us the best life ever. Much of our life is focused on making sure we live a great life. If someone asked us if we wanted to have the best life ever we would say, "Absolutely!" In this passage, Jesus gives us the way we can experience the best life ever; live life through Jesus. So often we spend so much of our time trying to find satisfaction in things that can never satisfy the way Jesus can. These things also can steal, kill and destroy us. Sometimes it is not the bad things that hurt our walk with God as much as the good things. If we are not careful we will look for the gifts of God to satisfy us in only a way that God can satisfy us. Today, rest in the fact that the greatest way to experience an amazing life is through an amazing savior Jesus Christ.

- How are you experiencing the full life Jesus promised?
- Is there anything in your life right know that might be stealing, killing or even destroying you? If so, repent from those things today.

TODAY'S CHALLENGE
Lord, thank you for the full life you have given me through Jesus Christ. Please help me live this life in the fullness that is you. Help me share this abundant life today with others who may not know you.

Steven Dunne • Minister to Students • Whitesburg Baptist Church, AL

• DAY 70 •

Take delight in the Lord, and he will give you the desires of your heart.
Psalm 37:4

I can remember the first time I read this verse. I was a high school student on a bus on the way to youth camp. I was so excited about this verse. I went to the front of the bus and asked my youth pastor, "Does this mean as long as I delight in the Lord I can have whatever I want?" "Not exactly," he replied. Then he began to explain what this verse really meant.

This verse doesn't mean if you delight in the Lord then you get a brand new car or a million dollars. This verse means something much greater then that. The psalmist is saying that when we truly delight in the Lord our heart becomes like His heart which will ultimately lead to our desires becoming His desires. When we delight in the Lord He might change what we desire in our hearts. As He changes what we desire in our hearts, our desires become the desires of His heart. There is great freedom in delighting in the Lord because what we learn is when our heart becomes his heart, and our desires become his desires we can ask for whatever we want. This is because we have gone through an amazing transformation; the kind of transformation that is only possible by the power of God.

So what does God desire? God desires that we know Him (John 17:3). God desires that we would glorify Him (1 Peter 4:11). God desires for the lost to be saved (2 Peter 3:9). God desires mercy (Hosea 6:6). These are just some of the things that God desires but the key is if we are ever going to desire the things he does then we must delight in Him. Some practical ways we can delight in God is by reading His Word, prayer, and worship. If you are not doing those things, then you are missing the riches that are truly available to Him. As you delight in the Lord and amazing thing begin to happen. You long for others to delight in Him also and you are willing to do whatever He calls you to so that others might delight in Him.

TODAY'S CHALLENGE
Lord, help me delight in you above everything and everyone else. As I delight in You make my heart like Your heart and make my desires Your desires.

Steven Dunne • Minister to Students • Whitesburg Baptist Church, AL

• DAY 71 •

In your relationships with one another, have the same mindset as Christ Jesus...he made himself nothing by taking the very nature of a servant, being made in human likeness.
Philippians 2:5-7

Assistant, attendant, helper and slave are all such perfect synonyms to the word "servant." Being a servant requires humility. Humility requires putting others before you. We live in a selfish world with generations becoming more and more about themselves. "It's all about ME!" is what the social media "selfie" is crying out. Why have we lost our grasp on the perfect example, which is that of Christ Jesus? Is it too difficult to put others before ourselves in our relationships?

- What relationships in your life lack humility?
- How can you show service to a friend or family member?

As a follower of Jesus, we are given a challenge to have the attitude of Christ. We know that the Bible gives us law to follow but why are we called to follow it? The reason we love is because He first loved us (1 John 4:19). In this same sense, we are to humble ourselves because he first humbled himself. Jesus did not want to have equality with God and have an advantage over man, which is why he came to the earth through incarnation. This allowed him to be "made in human likeness" and act as a servant. He was humbling himself by leaving heaven for earth which shows us the importance of putting others first.

It's not always easy to go out of our way for others. Maybe it's not always instinct to become a servant in any given situation. Humility is often a tough concept to grasp. One thing we know for sure. That is to "have the same mindset of Christ." Putting others before ourselves is not unattainable. We know this because Christ first showed us.

- Do others know how much you value their relationship? Is it because you see them as better than yourself?
- How are your conversations with others showing your humility? Do the conversations point more to the other person? Are you mainly talking about yourself?
- Continually ask God to give you the mindset of Christ so that others may be able to see Christ through your life.

TODAY'S CHALLENGE
Lord, show me how to reveal your humility through me. Help me to make it a point to put others before myself and see them as more important than me.

Joran Braughton • Student Pastor • Highland Baptist Church, OH

• DAY 72 •

A gentle answer turns away wrath, but a harsh word stirs up anger.
Proverbs 15:1

Defining the word "gentle" gives a clear meaning of being kind and admirable. These are great qualities to portray in a tough situation. Gentleness plays a great role not only in a person's character, but also their relationships. We can become angry at different times and it sure seems easier to give a harsh answer before a gentle one. But, after much research, it has been found that people tend to meet harsh words with even worse behavior. When we think a harsh or stern word is helping, it's only adding to the fire.

- Are you quicker to respond with a gentle or a harsh word?
- How many times have you been in a situation where harsh words were used? Would it have been different with a more gentle response?

Tony Dungy said, "People look more closely at our actions in the rough times, when the emotions are raw and our guard is down. That's when our true character shows and we find out our faith is real. If I'm going to call myself a Christian, I have to honor Jesus in the disappointments too." Sure, we may be angry or upset with each other. It's okay for that to happen, because it's in our human nature. God has given us a way out, though, and that way out is to have a gentle response. Responding in a way more like Jesus is more honoring than anything else. As a follower of Christ, we must point others toward him even in our conversations.

We must continue to demonstrate the love of Christ through our words in all conversation. No matter if we do this by speaking grace or by setting aside any anger or malice, we must show others Christ in us. (Ephesians 4:29; Colossians 3:8) This is how we must honor our God.

- How are your relationships with others, especially other followers of Jesus? Do your conversations display grace?
- Continually ask God to give you a gentle response in your conversations so that they will point others to Him.

TODAY'S CHALLENGE
Lord, allow me to show the gentleness and grace, which you have shown me. I want to display your character in every conversation and every relationship in my life.

Joran Braughton • Student Pastor • Highland Baptist Church, OH

• DAY 73 •

Jesus answered, "I am the way and the truth and the life.
No one comes to the Father except through me."
John 14:6

Wading the rivers of Alabama and Virginia, fishing has helped me find recreation and solace after tough days or weeks. It has also helped me find trouble at times. You see, the adventurer inside of me desires to trek further and further up unexplored creeks and coves, and I would often give in to that desire.

One crisp day on the New River, I traveled deeper than I had planned and decided to leave the water and find a shorter way back that didn't involve wading against the swift current. I found two paths. The first was smooth and free of bushes and trees. The second was a familiar walk, but would take more work to navigate the underbrush. I chose the route that looked easier, and spent hours wandering before eventually reaching my final destination.

Our world presents similar tempting paths to get us off the right way and onto the easy route. John 14:6 shows us how the path to the Father is a single lane. What Jesus declared here was a resounding shout to the false religions and idols of the world saying, "There is no way to God without the cross!"

The world tells us today that there is nothing that awaits us after life. It also tells us that all paths lead to the same destination. These lies have permeated our culture as people seek money, popularity, the perfect body and good works instead of heeding the truth outlined in these words of Christ. There is no fulfillment or salvation from following those roads. God's Word tells us that without Christ, there is no future. Our world offers so many wrong turns and roadblocks during our search for purpose in our lives, but we must remember our creator, his mission for our lives and the final destination that awaits those who follow Him. Everything worth living for begins and ends with Jesus.

TODAY'S CHALLENGE
"Father, help us become sold out in our love for you and our love for others. Please allow our love to overcome distractions from the enemy through your Holy Spirit. Help us point others to your son Jesus Christ. Protect us from idols that knock us from your path, and give us the passion to win others to your kingdom."

David Loyed • Minister to Middle School Students • Whitesburg Baptist Church, AL

• DAY 74 •

May these words of my mouth and this meditation of my heart
be pleasing in your sight, Lord, my Rock and my Redeemer.
Psalm 19:14

Throughout high school I remember vividly wanting to make my parents proud. I played in the marching band and always looked for them in the stands. I wrote for the student newspaper, and they were the first ones I showed my byline to. When my report card came out, I sought their approval. Deep in my heart, I desperately wanted to be pleasing in their sight. Unfortunately, high school contained way too many episodes where I wasn't very pleasing to my parents. I had times where my mouth got me in trouble, and my heart dwelt on things and schemes that weren't godly at all.

Think back upon the words that have slipped out of your mouth. Even worse, what about the thoughts that have darkened your mind? Are you thankful for God's grace and mercy yet? Romans 8:1 speaks to the believer and encourages us with the fact that, "...there is now no condemnation for those who are in Christ Jesus." The enemy seeks to incapacitate us with the sins of yesterday, but our God seeks to free us to carry out a spirit-filled life where the past has been put to rest.

Guilt over what we've said and done can swallow us alive, but God's provision says that we can be redeemed and renewed from our mistakes. David the Psalmist wrote of his desire to please the one who saved him. We should seek the same results as the psalmist. Our words and thoughts should glorify God. He is our rock in a world of sifting sand. We should remember daily that our Father seeks to guide us in our actions, but we must first give Him lordship over our lives.

TODAY'S CHALLENGE
Begin each day with the realization and resolve that you are the property of God who is our Rock and Redeemer. Give Him your thoughts and soak up His Word. Ask the Lord to allow the words and actions that flow from your spirit to be inspired by your Redeemer. Ask Him to take every thought captive and make you pleasing in His sight.

David Loyed • Minister to Middle School Students • Whitesburg Baptist Church, AL

• DAY 75 •

We are hard pressed on every side, but not crushed; perplexed, but not in despair;
persecuted, but not abandoned; struck down, but not destroyed.
2 Corinthians 4:8-9

"So we fix our eyes not on what is seen, but on what is unseen, since what is seen is temporary, but what is unseen is eternal" 2 Corinthians 4:16-18

Have you ever felt like life is just blindsiding you at times?
Ever get caught up in what's going on around you and lose sight where you are going?

The first passage talks about the fact that we as Christians are constantly attacked from every direction in their lives, yet somehow we make it through. Most Christians would admit we couldn't handle all that has happened or is going to happen in our lives by ourselves. Yet somehow we make it through each situation. It's Christ in us that brings us through. No matter what, life is going to happen. There's no stopping life. The thing to remember is that no matter what life throws at us God can handle it, plain and simple. As Christians, we have made Jesus king of our lives, and in doing so, the pressures and fears this world tries to throw at us are taken off our shoulders. Don't lose sight of God's plan for your life. There are things going on all around, you but keeping your eyes and heart focused on the Lord will bring you through.

"Do not fear, for I have redeemed you; I have summoned you by name; you are mine."
Isaiah 43:1

TODAY'S CHALLENGE
God give me eyes to see your plan and a heart willing to faithfully walk along side you through whatever you put before me.

Akil Mims • Minister in Residence • First Baptist Woodstock, GA

• DAY 76 •

The Lord had said to Abram, "Go from your country your people and your father's household to the land I will show you. I will make you into a great nation and I will bless you; I will make your name great, and you will be a blessing. I will bless those who bless you, and whoever curses you I will curse; and all peoples on earth will be blessed through you." So Abram went, as the Lord had told him, and Lot went with him. Abram was seventy-five years old when he set out from Harran.
Genesis 12:1-4

What has God been asking you to do?

Abram was 75 when God told him to leave his home, family, country, and also promised him a strong lineage. It wasn't until 25 years later that he even had the son God promised. That's a long time to wait. I know for me I sometimes struggle waiting for just five minutes. There are times when I feel like we struggle with patience for even some of the simplest things. At times, it may feel like we are aimlessly waiting. Yet, it's a good reminder that even when we feel like God is barely moving in certain areas of our lives He is still very much active in other parts of our lives. God has a plan. Oftentimes God wants to take us on a journey with a very real destination in mind. As we journey with Him, we gain experiences that prepare us for wherever or whatever He is leading us to. Never forget, patience isn't just stagnantly waiting for God it's also constantly walking with God.

Dear Lord, thank you so much for this day and the life you have given me. I know you have a purpose for all that You do. So I pray that you would give me kingdom focused eyes because honestly it's so easy for me to get distracted. Help me to make today all about what You want and to learn the lessons that You have placed before me. I know that if I just walk with You that in time You will make your plan known to me. I am so grateful for who You are and for who You have called me to be, through you. In Jesus name, Amen.

TODAY'S CHALLENGE
Remember that waiting isn't the same as doing nothing. God is always active in the lives of His followers.

Akil Mims • Minister in Residence • First Baptist Woodstock, GA

• DAY 77 •

The Word became flesh and made his dwelling among us. We have seen his glory, the
glory of the one and only Son, who came from the Father, full of grace and truth.
John 1:14

"Word" - Greek is logos, meaning word, spoken or written, often with a focus on the content of communication, matter, or thing. "The Word" is a title of Christ (John 1:1) emphasizing his own deity and communication of who God is and what he is like.
"Glory" - Greek is Doxa, translated with a wide range of meanings: the awesome light that radiates from God's presence and is associated with his acts of power, honor, praise, speaking of words of excellence and assigning highest status to God.

In this crazy world that we live in there are many times that we struggle and feel overwhelmed. In the midst of the struggles and overwhelming feeling that the world gives us we have a light, the Light, at the end of the tunnel. You see Jesus not only loves us and knows us, but He walked and lived (dwelled) among us. Jesus humbled Himself and lived with us. Jesus did not have to do that, but He did because he loves us. The truth of Jesus coming down from heaven to walk among us and show us love, grace, forgiveness, and truth is very encouraging and promising for us. Do you understand this? Do you see the greatness of this? Do you see the impact of this? Jesus was there at the beginning of creation!

TODAY'S CHALLENGE
Jesus humbled himself and came down from heaven to walk and live among us. Can you humble yourself and show this broken and hurting world the love that Christ showed us?

Joshua Singleton • Student • Southeastern Baptist Theological Seminary

• DAY 78 •

There is no fear in love. But perfect love drives out fear, because fear has to do with punishment. The one who fears is not made perfect in love. We love because he first loved us.
1 John 4:18-19

WOW!! Let's say that backwards, WOW!! Think about that for a minute. Better yet, read the passage again. Do you see that? Perfect love casts out fear.

This passage reveals to us that we have nothing to fear. Nothing that the world can throw at us should cause us to fear or be afraid. Think about that. With everything that the world can throw at you and everything that Satan does to try and cause us to take our eyes off of God, none of it can stand when love is present. That is a great promise and truth that we need to hold onto.

With the condition of America and the condition of the world, we have many things that could bring and cause fear, but because of the love that we receive from Christ, fear has no home or place in our life. Even with this promise there is still something greater that we are told. "We love because he first loved us." Do you understand that? The reason that we are able to love is because He first loved us. The reason that we are able to have fear of nothing is because He loved us first.

Think about that the next time you want to be afraid. Remember that we do not have to fear.

TODAY'S CHALLENGE
Allow Christ's love for us and your love for Christ to cast out fear and doubt. Demonstrate love to those that you encounter today.

Joshua Singleton • Student • Southeastern Baptist Theological Seminary

• DAY 79 •

Jesus Christ is the same yesterday and today and forever.
Hebrews 13:8

When I was in college, a few guys in my church group asked me if I'd be interested in filling in for one of their buddies on their intramural bowling team. I'm fairly sure that by now you are thinking one of two things: "I don't want to go to college where that guy went to college" or "They have intramural bowling?"

Truthfully, I really don't care for bowling (unless it's cosmic) and for whatever reason, I do not score well at bowling (seriously, my wife beats me down). Long story short, I bowled the game of my life. Somehow, I outscored all of the guys in my church group that invited me to play, and I led our team to victory in the process. What happens next? I never went back. Why? Because I knew the next time would not be the same. You may be thinking that I am shallow for letting my team down in this way, but hey, it's intramural bowling.

When we are inconsistent in our obedience and witness, others assume that we are just a "one-hit wonder" and our example cannot be trusted. The words, ways, and wonders of Jesus are not going anywhere; they never have and they never will. For our sakes, it is a great comfort to know that Jesus is always the same. His forgiveness is what you will receive every time you approach him with sincere confession. His desire for relationship with you will not vary. His fulfilling purpose for your life will be the same tomorrow as it is today. Because of this, He can be trusted with your future and with the standard for how you live.

TODAY'S CHALLENGE
Identify days, nights, or situations when your fellowship with the Lord is seriously challenged to remain consistent.

Andy John King • Student Pastor • Lindsay Lane Baptist Church, AL

• DAY 80 •

On hearing this, Jesus said, "It is not the healthy that need a doctor, but the sick."
Matthew 9:12

Jesus said the above because his disciples were asked the following question by the Pharisees: "Why does your teacher eat with tax collectors and sinners?" Jesus was hanging out with Matthew, a tax collector known for corruption and deceit. The Bible says in Matthew 9:10 that Jesus was also in the presence of many other notorious sinners while eating in the home of Matthew. Jesus, in all of his righteousness and glory, encourages his disciples to associate with and minister to reputable sinners.

My response to that is, "Thank goodness." Let us not forget that before Christ's presence in our lives, we too were reputable sinners. Because Christ loves enough to relate to the lost, we can be saved.

There is an obvious application that comes with this verse. Will you associate with and minister to the outcasts of your environment? Maybe it's the girl who is known for abusing drugs and remains quiet and distant from everyone or the popular guy that has only the reputation of causing trouble. More than likely, someone has come to your mind already.

Jesus didn't ignore or avoid those who were known for sin. He engaged them. Because He reaches out, we must reach out. If we have a relationship with Jesus, we have the cure for those suffering in sin.

TODAY'S CHALLENGE
Pray for the opportunity to associate with and minister to one or many that would come to mind while reading this devotion.

Andy John King • Student Pastor • Lindsay Lane Baptist Church, AL

• DAY 81 •

Let us not give up meeting together, as some are in the habit of doing, but let us encourage one another—and all the more as you see the Day approaching.
Hebrews 10:25

Community is at the heart of our faith. God created us not to be isolated beings, but to interact with others, to live in fellowship and to support one another. Twenty-first century culture, however, is geared more towards gadgets than personal interaction, and while an encouraging email or text message may lift our spirits when we need a boost, it doesn't replace the personal touch.

- Do you rely on technology when it comes to your relationships?
- Should you be creating more time in your schedule to meet others face to face?

Jesus doesn't want us to hide behind technology. He wants us to meet with others, to create authentic relationships and spread positive vibes and encouragement to those we encounter. After all, "Where two or three gather in my name, there am I with them" (Matthew 18:20). Whether we are meeting to worship, to have a coffee or to relax, everything we do can have an undercurrent of prayer. Jesus wants us to be involved and to approach everything with Christian values at the heart. It is when we show love, build trust and accompany people in their journeys of faith and life that we demonstrate true discipleship and care for others.

These values are also integral to effective student ministry. Young people are looking for role models, guidance and support as they approach adulthood. By taking a real interest in them, giving opportunities for them to meet others, providing a safe space and a chance to develop skills we are modeling true authentic relationships with Christian values at the very core. Having the ability to celebrate successes and challenge appropriately can inspire our friends and family to deepen their faith and share their gifts and talents freely with others.

- Which communities are you part of? How can you be more actively involved?
- Do you know anyone who would appreciate some encouragement? How can you help? Meet with them informally and find out.

TODAY'S CHALLENGE
Lord, allow me to encourage others each day. Help me to share my values and talents with everyone I meet and to be a true witness to your love.

Katharine O'Brien • Catechetical and Youth Co-ordinator • Our Lady of Lourdes, London UK

• DAY 82 •

Trust in the LORD with all your heart and lean not on your own understanding. In all your ways acknowledge him, and he will make your paths straight.
Proverbs 3:5-6

Entering into a relationship with God is a lifelong process that can sometimes take tremendous courage. When things are looking bleak, God is there and in control. This is something that we, as followers of Jesus, may forget.

- What are the challenges in your life?
- Are there any barriers preventing you from inviting God fully into your situation?

As a follower of Jesus, you are never truly alone. God wants to be there for you through everything and to be fully involved in your life. You are invited to "cast all your anxiety on him because he cares for you" (1Peter 5:7). This, for some of us, involves a real leap of faith. We make ourselves completely vulnerable when, in the midst of struggles, we look beyond our own judgment. We can do this through honest conversations with God. Allowing him to take control can bring about real peace and a new sense of perspective. Confiding in Jesus as a trusted friend, as part of our daily routine, will enable us to navigate challenges more easily and progress in our own spiritual journey and prayer life.

During my ministry, I have greatly valued having a strong support network. Christian living is far from easy. Having supportive people on our side provides opportunities to share life's experiences, celebrating and challenging where appropriate. In order to be authentic disciples for young people, we need to insure our own needs are fully explored and met. This spiritual accompaniment can inspire us to take courage and continue our walk with God, despite difficult circumstances. Involvement in ministry does not make us "God experts," but by trusting and dedicating our service to Him, we can find our way through the storms of life and seek to use our gifts and talents to their full potential.

Do you have the courage to let God help? Start an honest conversation with Him today. Is there a friend or relative whose faith journey inspires you? Invite them to join your support network.

TODAY'S CHALLENGE
Lord, help me to be courageous in faith. Allow me to communicate freely with you, trust you whole-heartedly and draw on the support of others to guide me.

Katharine O'Brien • Catechetical and Youth Co-ordinator • Our Lady of Lourdes, London UK

• DAY 83 •

*The Lord said to me, "Go, show your love to your wife again, though
she is loved by another man and is an adulteress."*
Hosea 3:1-2

It would be appropriate to suggest that a true test of love may include the following two questions: To what extent are you willing to go to demonstrate your love? How much are you willing to give up in order to prove it?

The answers from Jesus' perspective towards the lost would say: All the way. Everything.

Besides Jesus, the story of Hosea and his wife Gomer demonstrate a powerful picture of love that is pressed into action. In the midst of adultery on Gomer's part, Hosea is commanded by God to seek out his wife to love her again. The command to "Go again" in verse 1 suggests that this is possibly not even the first time Hosea has had to do so. Very few could imagine the throbbing pain of intentionally seeking out an adulterous spouse in order to restore a marriage.

Verse 2 deepens the love extent as Hosea has found Gomer in the city square on an auction block. Gomer's adulterous life has been marginalized to the point of being sold as a slave. While many could find satisfaction in Gomer's plight, Hosea finds compassion. At the last moment, Hosea offers everything he has in order to bring Gomer home.

The parallel to Jesus is striking. Even from the Old Testament story of Hosea and Gomer, the extent to which Jesus would be willing to go and to give up for a lost and rebellious world would be demonstrated and foreshadowed hundreds of years prior to his arrival on earth. The fact that God commanded Hosea to find his wife again compounds the abiding desire of Christ in pursuing a lost world.

The story of Hosea and Gomer, indeed Jesus' mission as well, could be summarized by the following statements: Love is willing to go. Love is willing to pay.

The question for the redeemed of Christ becomes, "What could possibly hinder my invitation to the lost world on behalf of Jesus?"

TODAY'S CHALLENGE
Would you ask God today for the opportunity to speak the name of Jesus to someone and to offer a simple invitation to come to church with you?

Matt Lawson • Student Pastor • First Baptist Woodstock, GA

91

• DAY 84 •

Blessed are you when people insult you, persecute you and falsely say all kinds of evil against you because of me. Rejoice and be glad, because great is your reward in heaven, for in the same way they persecuted the prophets who were before you.
Matthew 5:11-12

History narrates the stories of many Christians who lived a life of faith and gave their lives so others can know the gospel. One of those was Jim Elliot, known by many as one of the five missionaries martyred by jungle Indians in Ecuador 50 years ago. Consider some of the following thoughts that he penned before his death...

"He is no fool who gives what he cannot keep to gain that which he cannot lose."

"God, I pray Thee, light these idle sticks of my life and may I burn for Thee. Consume my life, my God, for it is Thine. I seek not a long life, but a full one, like you, LORD Jesus."

"We are so utterly ordinary, so commonplace, while we profess to know a Power the Twentieth Century does not reckon with. But we are "harmless," and therefore unharmed. Meekness must be had for contact with men, but brass, outspoken boldness is required to take part in the comradeship of the Cross. The world cannot hate us; we are too much like its own. Oh that God would make us dangerous!"

I once heard a missionary say that the blood of martyrs is the fertilizer for new church plants. I have a missionary friend who recently went to the exact spot where Jim Elliot was killed to celebrate the 50 year anniversary of his death. During that celebration, Auca Indians were baptized in the same river where the blood of these five young men once flowed from being speared to death. The man that killed the missionaries is now preaching around the world at conferences telling others how Christ saved him. Only God can do something like that!

What prevents you today from being vocal about your faith? Is it fear, doubt, worldliness, persecution or maybe something else? Let today be an opportunity to find joy in the journey by expressing your love for Jesus to someone.

TODAY'S CHALLENGE

Say this out loud right now: I am more afraid of not doing what God called me to do than doing that which pleases me. Close your personal devotion time in prayer asking God to help you remember that his love is for all people and help you to show his love to all with whom you come in contact.

Matt Lawson • Student Pastor • FBC Woodstock, GA

• DAY 85 •

For to me, to live is Christ and to die is gain
Philippians 1:21

Sometimes we go through life living in our own selfish wants and desires. We forget we have life because Christ is alive. To live, plainly means "to continue to be alive." We as believers could not continue to be alive without the sacrifice of Jesus Christ.

- What are you living for?
- Have you forgotten today that your life isn't your own?

It may sound like we *have* to give up everything. We might even dread the sound of giving up our lives. Let's switch up the perspective here in the way that Philippians states "to die is to gain." Death is a great loss in a worldly view, for we lose all of our earthly comforts and all our hopes. But for a believer, it is gain. It is the end of all weakness and misery. Live with hope in view of death, because Christ is our purpose in death. We *get* to give up everything because we gain all that we need in Jesus Christ. Giving up everything can be in the sense of giving Jesus our time, allowing our dreams to focus on His purpose, and following Him in obedience.

TODAY'S CHALLENGE
Allow God to take your life in the palm of His hands, so that your death will be gain in the arms of our Savior.

Lane Taylor • Minister in Residence • First Baptist Woodstock, GA

• DAY 86 •

I am the vine; you are the branches. If you remain in me and I in you, you will bear much
fruit; apart from me you can do nothing.
John 15:5

A vine is a plant that grows along the ground or up and around something. The branches of a vine are defined as something that extends from or enters into a main body or source. In John 15:5, it states, "I am the vine; you are the branches." He is the main source, we as the branches need to be able to grow in Him alone. If we are not daily taking in from the main source, we sit still as dead branches that do not bear fruit.

- Are you seeking Him in your life daily?
- What is your vine that you're trying to bear fruit from?

We must realize that we as believers cannot fulfill our purpose on this earth. As stated in Mathew 28:19 "Go therefore and make disciples of all nations, baptizing them in the name of the Father and of the Son and of the Holy Spirit." Apart from Christ, we cannot and will not bear fruit from our vine. We must abide in Jesus Christ alone. The phrase "abiding in Christ" illustrates a close and intimate relationship with Jesus Christ. This is evident by living in obedience to Christ's commands, following Jesus' example, and living free from habitual sin.

TODAY'S CHALLENGE
Lord, please be the source of my life. I choose to abide in you daily; knowing without you, I can do nothing.

Lane Taylor • Minister in Residence • First Baptist Woodstock, GA

• DAY 87 •

For what I received I passed on to you as of first importance : that Christ died for our sins according to the Scriptures, that he was buried, that he was raised on the third day according to the Scriptures,
1 Corinthians 15:3-4

Whatever is most important to you is what drives everything you do. Ask yourself that question, "What really is absolutely most important to me?" This second question is even more important to ask yourself. "What really is most important?" In this passage, God has told us the most important part of all life is the Gospel!

The Gospel is the most important part of all life because it grants us a relationship with God, by it God blesses our lives, and from it God gives us eternal life.

The final question to focus on today is, "What is the Gospel?" Take a moment and write what you believe the Gospel is. Be careful not to put too much in or take too much out.

The easiest way to remember the real Gospel is this simple statement "The Gospel is the **PoWeR** of Jesus." Let's focus on the P, W, and R to define the Gospel.

P: The **Person** of Jesus. The Gospel's power is through Jesus being God the Son, becoming the ultimate human, and eternally being our death and life.

W: The **Work** of Jesus. The Gospel's power is also through Jesus living sinlessly, dying sacrificially for our sin, and rising eternally.

R: Our **Response** to Jesus. The Gospel's power is finally through our repentance of sin and faithfully following Him (Jesus).

TODAY'S CHALLENGE
Give your life to Jesus through the Gospel if you have not already. If you have already, then live the gospel by humbly repenting of sin and faithfully following Him.

Chip Dean • Middle School Pastor • First Baptist Woodstock, GA

• DAY 88 •

And beginning with Moses and all the Prophets, he explained to them what was said in all the Scriptures concerning himself.
Luke 24:27

Let's be honest, there are many people who don't have a consistent devotional life because they don't understand the Bible. In fact, you might even find the Bible to be boring, confusing, and little to do with your life. But if God really wrote the Bible for all people to come to know Him, then should He really have written it in a better way? God is perfect and can't do anything less than perfect, so His Word is perfect and is exactly what we need for our life.

Since the Bible is perfect, we must then admit that we are not. What could we do as imperfect people to understand God's perfect Word better for life change? In today's verse, Jesus gives us the way to understand His Word. He was on a walk with two of His disciples. He talked them through the entire Old Testament. He showed them how everything in the Bible is all about Him.

Many people read the Bible as if it was all about them to have a better life or to know more truth to get them through their day. That's why they find the Bible so boring. All of life and Scripture is not about us, but it's all about Jesus. He is where we find our joy, identity, purpose, and understanding.

TODAY'S CHALLENGE

- Let every Biblical character you come across, good or evil, remind you of your need for the perfect Jesus.
- Let every Biblical story you read about, show you the need for the gospel of Jesus.
- Let every truth and command you read, show you the need to know and live for Jesus.

Chip Dean • Middle School Pastor • First Baptist Woodstock, GA

• DAY 89 •

At this, Job got up and tore his robe and shaved his head. Then he fell to the ground in worship and said: "Naked I came from my mother's womb, and naked I will depart. The Lord gave and the Lord has taken away; may the name of the Lord be praised." In all this, Job did not sin by charging God with wrongdoing.
Job 1:20-22

Job experienced trial after trial throughout his life. After his house was destroyed and some of his children were killed, he fell to the ground and worshipped God, blessing His name. This reaction is not typical for most people. Job had completely put his trust in the Lord and knew that God was in control. Everything that we have is truly from the Lord, and it is his decision to give or take it. We should rejoice at both. Our joy is to be found only in the Almighty God, not in material possessions or in relationships with other people.

Barbara Youderian's husband, Roger, was killed by the Auca Indians along with Jim Elliott and three other men. In her journal, Barbara wrote, "As I came face to face with the news of Roj's death my heart was filled with praise. He was worthy of his home going." Only when our strength comes from God can we praise Him at the death of a loved one.

Both Job & Barbara were able to give God the glory by the examples they set. Job went through more trials than anyone of us could imagine, yet he continued to bless the Lord. Barbara, in the midst of sorrow, had a heart filled with praise. She knew that she and her husband were faithful to what God had called them to.

The way we handle struggles and trials is a testimony of whom we trust. When we put our trust in God and realize that everything we have is from Him, then we will be able to praise Him all the time. As we strive to become totally dependent on the Lord, we will be able to bless His name when we experience difficult times. Our joy and our strength are found in the Father.

TODAY'S CHALLENGE
Make a list of 50 things you are grateful for & then reflect on them when you are in the middle of a trial.

Laura Lawson • Ministry Assistant • Student Ministry Sidekick

• DAY 90 •

*Charm is deceptive and beauty is fleeting; but a woman who
fears the Lord is to be praised.*
Proverbs 31:30

True beauty is an inward beauty, not an outward expression. Jesus' death on the cross paid the penalty for our sins. We have been cleansed by the blood of Jesus and now we are white as snow. The way we carry ourselves, dress, and behave should be a reflection of the inner change that has taken place. We are to be a living testimony to unbelievers. Women, especially, should be conscious of the message they send out. The motives should be pure when we decide what to wear for the day. When people see you, they should not see your clothes but instead attention should be brought to the Lord. In all that we do we should bring glory and honor to Him.

Focusing on the idea of presenting our bodies before God will help us in our relationship with our Father. We should desire to be more like Jesus. As we renew our minds by mediating and studying His Word daily, we are learning more about Him. As our knowledge of God increases, our faith and fear will increase too. When we fear God our daily life will be a reflection of our respect and awe of Him. The fear that we have for the Lord will overflow into our decisions and actions. True beauty is becoming more like Christ & fearing the Lord!

TODAY'S CHALLENGE
Prayerfully ask God to show you areas in your life that you are not honoring Him and then ask God to help you in those areas.

Laura Lawson • Ministry Assistant • Student Ministry Sidekick

• CONTRIBUTING AUTHORS •

Aaron T. Colyer, Student Pastor, MacArthur Boulevard Baptist Church Aaron has a passion to see teenagers trust and follow Christ who lead others to trust and follow Christ! He has been a guest blogger at TGM (Theology Gospel Mission) and youthgrouptruth.com. He makes his home in Dallas, TX with his amazing wife and three great kids. Follow him on Twitter: @atcolyer

Akil Mims, Minister-in-Residence, First Baptist Woodstock
Akil loves to share who Jesus is with teenagers. He graduated from Kennesaw State University in 2012 and now attends New Orleans Baptist Theological Seminary. His love for student ministry feeds into his desire to constantly learn how to better make and equip disciples. @akilmims

Alan Ostrzycki, Student Pastor (Children/Jr. High), Lindsay Lane Baptist
Alan has been in student ministry for 7 years. He served as a primary initiator and current board member for First Priority of North Alabama, a local organization that has established intentionally evangelistic clubs in over 20 schools in North Alabama, which equips and empowers students to be missionaries on their campus. Alan lives in Athens, AL with his wife of three years, Rebecca, and their two year old son, Cooper.

Andy John King, Campus Pastor and Student Pastor, Lindsay Lane Baptist Church
Andy John is currently serving as campus pastor for the east campus of Lindsay Lane Baptist Church in Athens, Alabama. He also serves as Lindsay Lane's senior high and college student pastor. Andy John and his wife Britney live in Athens with their two children, Davis and Noelle. @LLStudentPastor

Ben Hyrne, Student Pastor, Calvary Baptist Church
Ben has been serving in full-time ministry in the rural suburbs of Atlanta for over a year. During that time he's been active in the public schools; participating in their weekly bible studies and serving as the chaplain for a high school football team. Ben just celebrated his third wedding anniversary with his beautiful wife Emory. @BenHyrne

B.J. Cobb, Associate Pastor, Northside Baptist Church
BJ has 13 years of experience in leading student ministry and recently received his M.Div. from New Orleans Baptist Theological Seminary. His philosophy of student ministry includes equipping parents to make disciples of their children. BJ and his wife Lindsey have three children, Micah, Joshua, and Hannah, and are expecting their fourth child in 2014. @BJCobb56

Chad Williams, Minister to Students and Families, Tabernacle Baptist Church
Chad has been a student minister for 12 years and also serves with International World Changers to send teenagers around the world on international mission trips every summer. Chad currently lives in Decatur, IL with his wife Jennifer and boys, Nate and Peyton. @chadwilliams78

Chase Allen, Minister to Families, Northside Baptist Church
Chase is passionate about seeing teens come to know Jesus. He and his wife Taylor live in Orangeburg, SC and they are expecting their first son Noah in December. He also loves to hunt and watch Alabama football. @Chase5allen

Chip Dean, Middle School Pastor, First Baptist Church Woodstock, GA
Chip has been in youth ministry for over a decade. His greatest passion is to see students understand the storyline of the Scriptures in a Christ-centered, gospel-grounded, and life-changing way. You can check out his free resources such as a mega-series through the whole Bible and a mega-series through all of doctrine for students at www.youth-grouptruth.com.
@ChipDean

Chris Fedorcek, Young Adults Pastor, Sanctuary of Ocala
Chris is the author of Culture Crisis and is presently working on his second book. He currently resides in Ocala, FL with his wife Rachel and their two children, Emma and Nicklaus. @chrisfedorcek

Chris Rainey, Associate and Student Pastor, Liberty Baptist Church
Chris has served in a leadership role in student ministries in Georgia and Texas for over 10 years. His desire is see students become disciples who make disciples by owning and sharing their faith. Chris currently lives in Chatsworth, GA with his wife, Lindsey, and daughter, Addie. @crainey1984

Chuck Jonas, Pastor of Worship and Students, Reidsville Baptist Church
Chuck has been in ministry for over 20 years. Chuck has led leadership training in the areas of Sunday School and Vacation Bible School throughout the state of Georgia. Chuck lives in Reidsville, an hour west of Savannah, with his wife Lanie and daughter Rachel. @chuck5363

Daniel Peavy, Student and Discipleship Pastor, First Baptist Church Daniel has served in Student Ministry for over 10 years. He is an avid Atlanta Braves and UGA Football Fan. Daniel lives in Jackson, Georgia with his wife Megan and their daughter Erin. @bigdaddypeave

David Loyed, Minister to Middle School Students, Whitesburg Baptist Church
David spent ten years in the business world before answering God's call to ministry at 28. He lives in Huntsville, Alabama with his wife Joyce and kids, Mason, Matthew, and Faith. @davidloyed @theburgstudents

David O'Dell, Pastor, Hardy Street Baptist Church
David is passionate about biblical preaching. David received his D.Min from NOBTS in Leadership and Administration. David lives in Hattiesburg, Mississippi with his wife Heather and their four children Carter, Summer, Tilly, and Story. @davemo44

David Richardson, Associate Pastor Youth/Missions, First Baptist Creedmoor
David lives in Creedmoor, North Carolina with his wife Becky and two adopted sons, Josh and Nate. He just finished Seminary at Liberty University – Go Flames! @revdrichardson

Dustin Sams, Student Pastor, Second Baptist Conway, AR
Dustin has been serving as a student pastor for more than 20 years. Served on Super Summer Arkansas Leadership for 10 years and has been a guest speaker at numerous conferences and youth events. Dustin lives in Conway, Arkansas with his wife Erika and children Dalton and Sammy Jo.

Greg Schmid, Teen Development Director, Bob Temple Northside YMCA
Greg has been in student ministry for 25 years, working with at risk teens and students that have trouble just fitting in. Greg has been married to Robin for 26 years and is the dad of three kids, Kayla, Karlie, and Keely. They live in Corryton, outside of Knoxville, Tn. @gregschmid07

Jason Dorriety, Student Pastor, Spring Valley Baptist Church Jason is a veteran student minister with a passion to see students and families experience Christ in their daily lives. Jason lives in Columbia, SC with his wife Ann and kids, Betsy and Will. @jasondorriety

Jason Mitchell, Pastor of Outreach and New Initiatives, First Baptist Springfield
Jason loves leading students and adults to reach out to their neighbors and to the nations with the gospel. He lives in northern Virginia with his awesome wife Lilli and his cool kids, Ada, Izzy, JD, and Jesse. @JasonEMitchell

Jay Smith, Associate Pastor of Youth & Education, Screven Baptist Church
Jay lives in Georgetown, SC with his wife, Beth, and their three girls: Jillian, Kirstan, and Bryleigh. His favorite verse in Philippians 3:10, "That I may know Him, and the power of His resurrection, and the fellowship of His sufferings, being made conformable unto His death." @pastorjaysmith

Jeff Walker, Pastor of Students, First Baptist Church of Gray Gables
A Northeast Florida native, Jeff loves the Lord, loves his wife Jennifer, loves his kids, Luke, Abram, & Sawyer, and loves teaching and ministering to students. He is passionate about helping students form a firm foundation of faith by walking them through the scriptures, verse by verse. Jeff occasionally writes at his blog: www.Jeffsspeakage.wordpress.com.

Jesse Payne, Student Pastor, Lakeland Baptist Church As a former NCAA Division 1 shortstop in baseball, Jesse loves Jesus and all things sports. He lives in the Dallas/Ft. Worth Metroplex, and is a graduate of UT-Arlington and is currently pursuing his Master of Divinity from Southwestern Baptist Theological Seminary. @jmpayne12

Jody Livingston, Youth Pastor, Kennesaw First Baptist Church
Jody oversees Middle and High School ministries. Jody lives just outside of Atlanta with his wife Sarah and kids, Emma, Anna, Lizzy, and Jack. He also owns a sweet 1972 VW Beetle. @jodylivingston

John Grigsby, Sunday School Director, Graveston Baptist Church John has been involved with youth ministry for over 15 years. He is the creator of Blackberry Wisdom www.johndgrigsby.com. John lives outside Knoxville, TN with his wife Cindy and kids, Danielle and Austin. @jdgrigsby

Joran Braughton, Student Pastor, Highland Baptist Church
Joran has a passion to make disciples of students who go and make disciples of others. After growing up in Ohio, he went on to graduate from Liberty University in 2011. He has spent the last two years living in Woodstock, Ga. @joranbraughton

Josh Reid, Student Pastor, First Baptist Cary, NC
Josh desires to lead this generation of students in living out the Gospel each day, equipping them to lead those around them. He enjoys writing, music and doing ministry with his wife, Jacqueline. @joshuamarkreid

Joshua D. Singleton, Student, Southern Baptist Theological Seminary
I am pursuing a M. Div with an emphasis in Youth and Family Ministry at Southern Baptist Theological Seminary. I have been in student ministry for over 10 years. I love reading comics, drawing, and spending time with family and friends. @jd_singleton

Katharine O'Brien, Catechetical and Youth Co-ordinator, Our Lady of Lourdes Catholic Church, Wanstead, London UK.
Katharine is a professionally qualified youth worker taking on a new role in parish youth ministry. She has youth work experience in both secular and faith based settings, including the Brentwood Catholic Youth Service retreat centre, Walsingham House. Katharine is also studying for an MA in Pastoral Ministry, focusing on the faith development of young people. @katharine_adair

Katie Jones, Minister-in-Residence, First Baptist Woodstock
Katie is a recent Bible college graduate and is passionate about girls ministry. After graduation, she moved from South Carolina to Colorado to work with students in the heart of Boulder. She is now living and working in Georgia. @knjones830

Kent Bjurstrom, Pastor of Student Ministries, Sugar Grove Church
Kent has been in student ministry for six years in a rural community in Indiana. He enjoys Diet Coke, sports, speaking, writing (pastorkentb.com), playing guitar & hanging out with middle school and high school students. Kent loves life with his wife Stephanie and three boys, Trey, Colby & Cayden. @pastorkentb

Lane Taylor, Minister-in-Residence, First Baptist Woodstock
Lane has a heart for Girls Ministry, a passion God has laid on her heart to encourage girls to serve God by building relationships based on the love that God showed her in her life. She is in enrolled at Liberty University Online studying Religion and Counseling. @Lanetaytay

Laura Lawson, Ministry Assistant, Student Ministry Sidekick
Laura has a passion for her family, teenage girls, history and travel. She graduated from The College at Southeastern with a degree in Biblical Studies. She lives outside of Atlanta with her husband Matt and two children, Deacon & Eden. @lauralawson25

Lee Clamp, Director of Evangelism, South Carolina Baptist Convention
Lee is a missional catalyst among 2100 Baptist churches. He assists church leaders as they motivate the church to move from the sanctuary to the streets to give each person far from God an ongoing opportunity to see, hear, and respond to the Gospel. He is the creator of the One initiative and speaks in a variety of settings throughout South Carolina. Lee lives in Lexington, SC with his wife Leisa and three sons Caden, Connor, and Corder. @leeclamp

Lloyd Blank, Student Pastor, Ridgecrest Baptist Church Lloyd has spent the better part of 20 years serving in various student ministry roles. In 2005, after serving in mostly bi-vocational positions, he left a management position with a Fortune 500 company to take his first full-time student pastor position. He currently resides in Dothan AL with his wife Stephania. They have two children Kayla & Brian. @lloydblank

Matt Lawson, Student Pastor, First Baptist Woodstock
Matt is the author of Twisdom as well as a contributing author to three other books. He's the creator of StuminSidekick.com, a site dedicated to resourcing youth ministry leaders. Matt lives just outside Atlanta with his wife Laura and kids, Deacon and Eden. @mattlawson77

Matt Sawyer, Student Pastor, Southside Baptist Church
I am humbled to be on this adventure with my wife Chelsea and my girls, Addison and Presley. When I'm not hanging out with my girls I enjoy running, reading, playing music, and coffee. I'm excited to see what God does through this resource! @matt_sawyer

Mike D'Attoma, Student Pastor, First Baptist Barnwell
Mike has been in student ministry for nearly 10 years, and has a deep passion for discipleship and God's Word. His passion is to see families growing together in the grace of the Gospel. He is an avid sports fan, and loves THE Ohio State University. He lives in Barnwell, SC with his wife, Sarah, and their beautiful daughter, Camila. @mikedattoma

Patrick Stalnaker, Pastor to Students and Families, First Baptist Kettering
Patrick has served in student ministry for 15+ years in Florida, North Carolina, South Carolina and now Ohio leading worship, preaching and discipling students to a deeper walk with Christ. Patrick lives in Kettering, Ohio with his wife Anne and kids Addie, Carson and Brayden. Follow him on Twitter at @pdstalnaker.

Robby Lewis, Student Pastor, The Journey Church
Robby is a graduate of Liberty University with a passion for seeing students KNOW Christ Personally, GROW with Christ Intimately and SHOW Christ Passionately. Robby lives in Fernandina Beach, Florida with his bride Cecily and son Canon.

Ryan West, Student Pastor, First Baptist McGehee
Ryan is an avid sports fan, and combines this passion with his love of Christ, to communicate to students and adults. Ryan is passionate about seeing the Gospel transform lives in people of all ages. Ryan lives in Southeast Arkansas with his wife, Ra'Shele, and his son Sylas. @r8west

Scott Huff, Student Pastor, Coastal Community Church
Scott is a student pastor and a camp pastor for Lifeway's FUGE camps, disciple now weekends, school chapel services, and other events. He also writes a ministry blog at www.scotthuffblog.wordpress.com. Scott lives in Charleston, SC with his wife, Lori. @scotthuff

Shane Newton, Student Pastor, Southside Baptist Church
Shane has been serving in youth ministry for thirteen years. Shane lives in Andalusia, Alabama with his wife Anna and two kids, Britany and Dylan. @Shane_Newton1

Stephen Fountain, Student Pastor, First Baptist Buford
Stephen is 29 years old and in his tenth year of student ministry. He has a passion for speaking to students and a love for campus ministry birthed from his belief that school campuses are the greatest mission fields in America. Stephen lives just north of Atlanta with his wife Erin and daughter Emma. @StephenFountain

Steven Dunne, Minister to Students, Whitesburg Baptist Church
Steven Is the minister to Students at Whitesburg Baptist Church. He has been blessed to serve on staff here the Last ten years. Steven lives in Huntsville, Alabama and has been married to his wife Elizabeth for the last nine years. They have 2 amazing daughters Anna Faith and Ellie Grace.